Baltica

Coloring book inspired by Lithuanian folk art

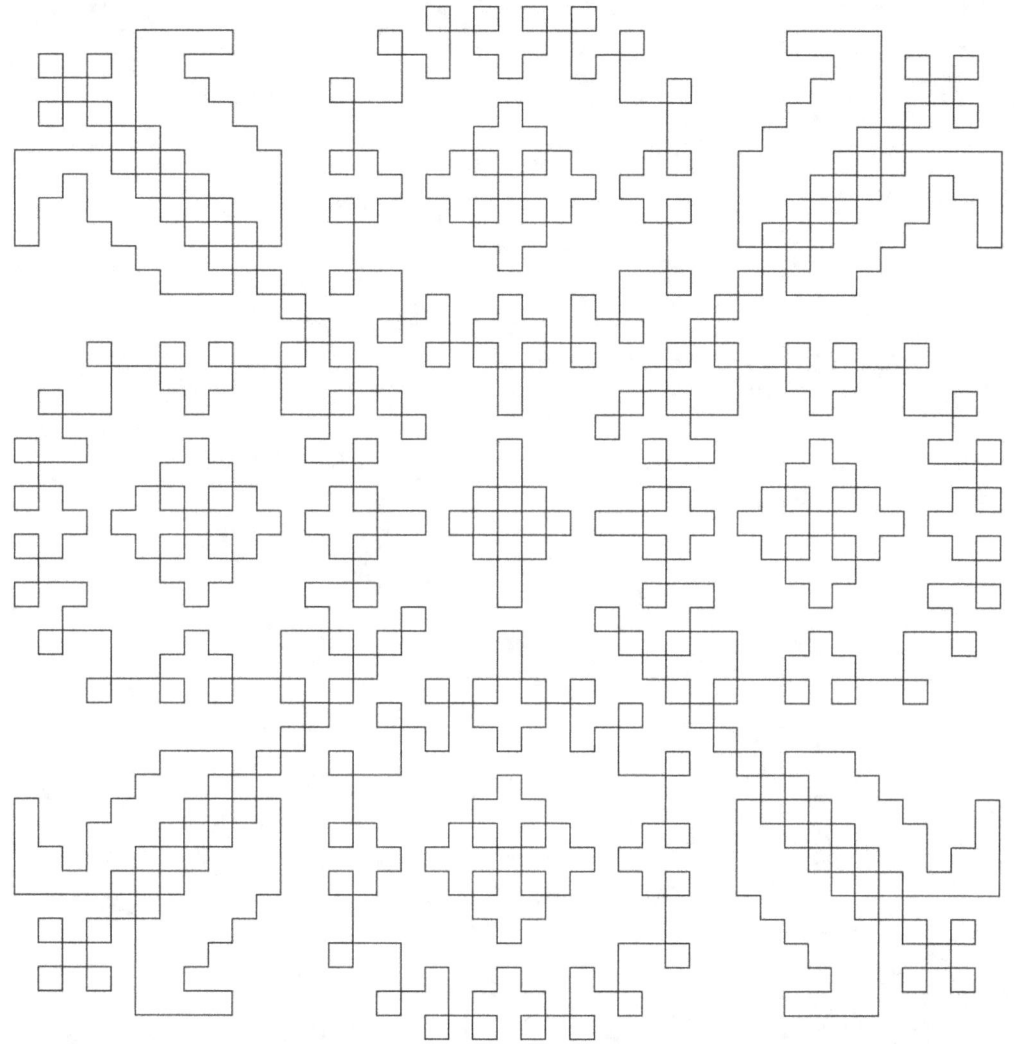

Baltica Volume V , Second edition, Copyright © 2025 Alice Koko. All rights reserved.

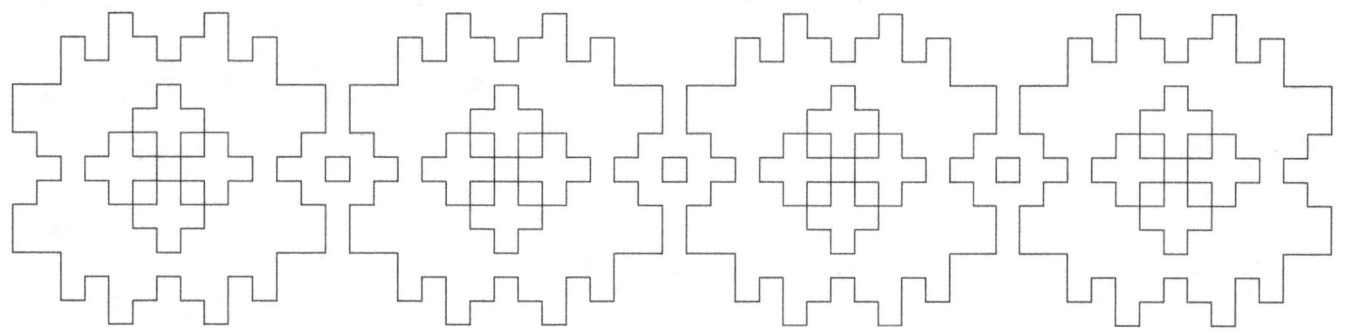

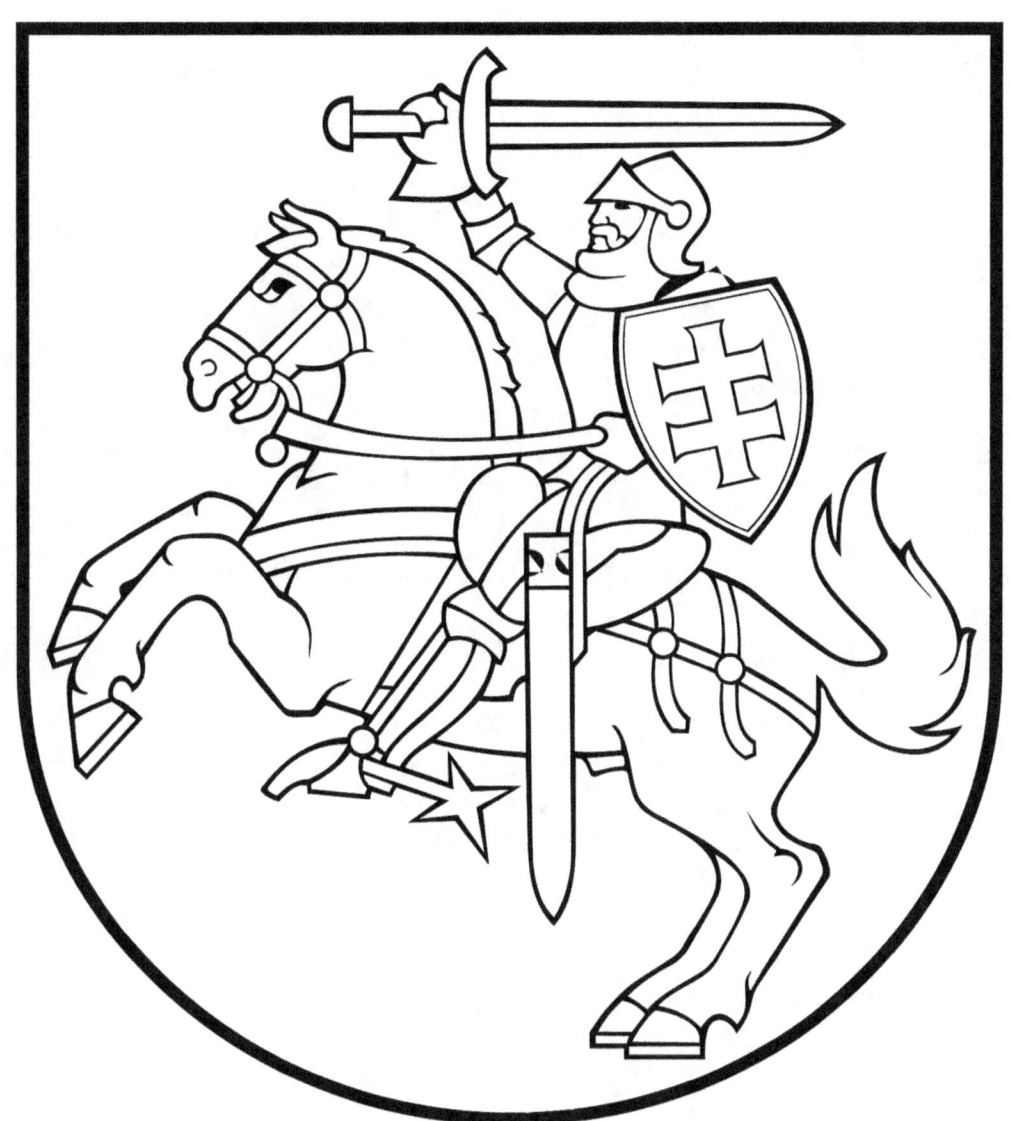

Lithuania is a Baltic state in northern-eastern Europe; it is situated along
the southeastern shore of the Baltic Sea, to the east of Sweden and Denmark.
It is bordered by Latvia to the north, Belarus to the east and south,
Poland to the south, and Kaliningrad Oblast to the southwest.
The official language, Lithuanian, along with Latvian, is one of only two living
languages in the Baltic branch of the Indo-European language family and
amongst the European languages, Lithuanian is closest in grammar to Sanskrit.
Vilnius is the capital of Lithuania and recognized by UNESCO as one of the most
beautiful cities of the Old Continent with the largest Baroque old town in Eastern and
Central Europe; interestingly, the Vilnius Baroque was built on medieval foundations.
The geographic centre of Europe is 26 km north of Vilnius.
Lithuania is renowned for its beautiful folk art in textiles; weaving, crochet and knitwear.
Cherished handicraft traditions are honored and passed on for generations.
Here's a little glimpse into the beauty of the Lithuanian folk art.
Enjoy!

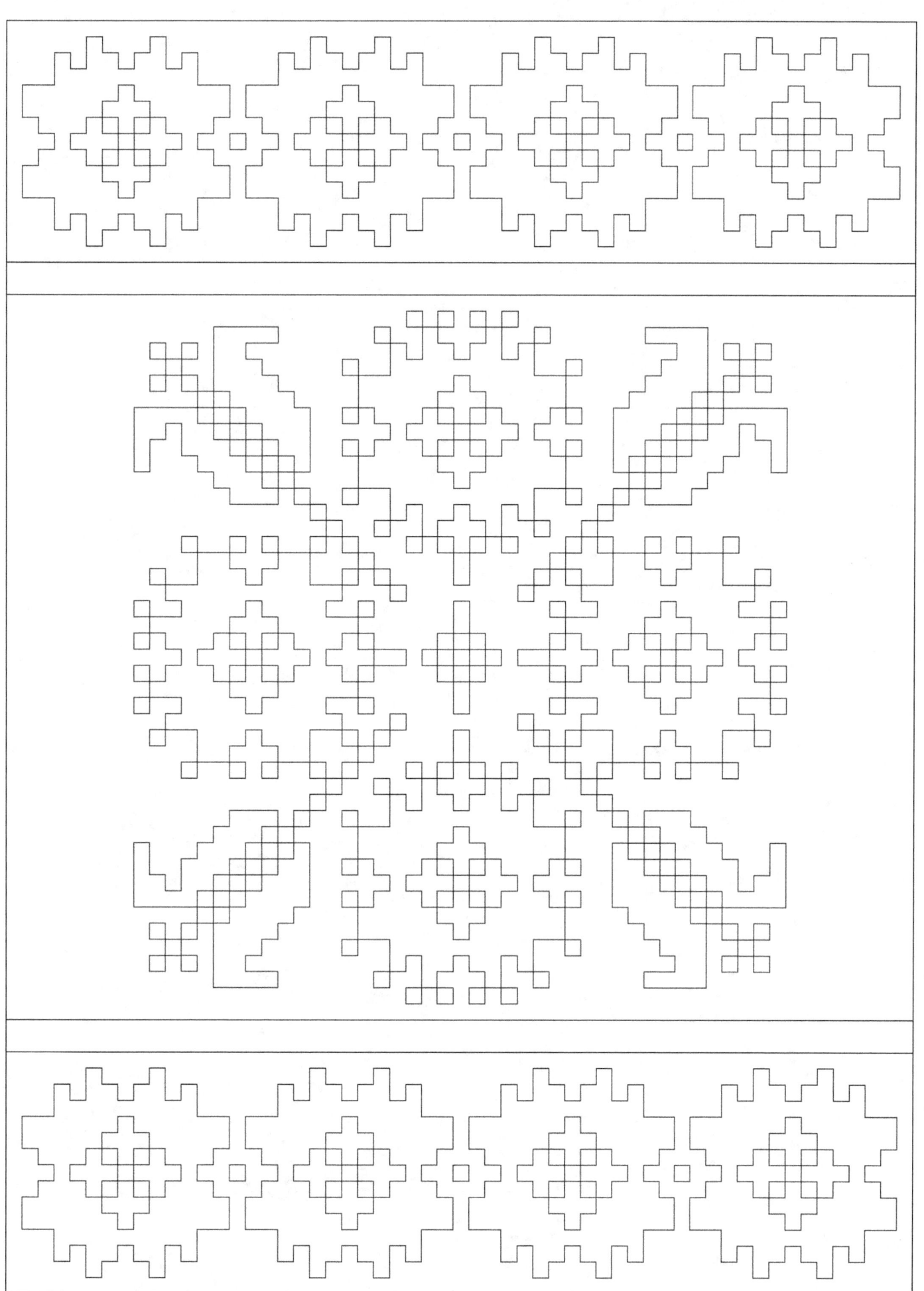

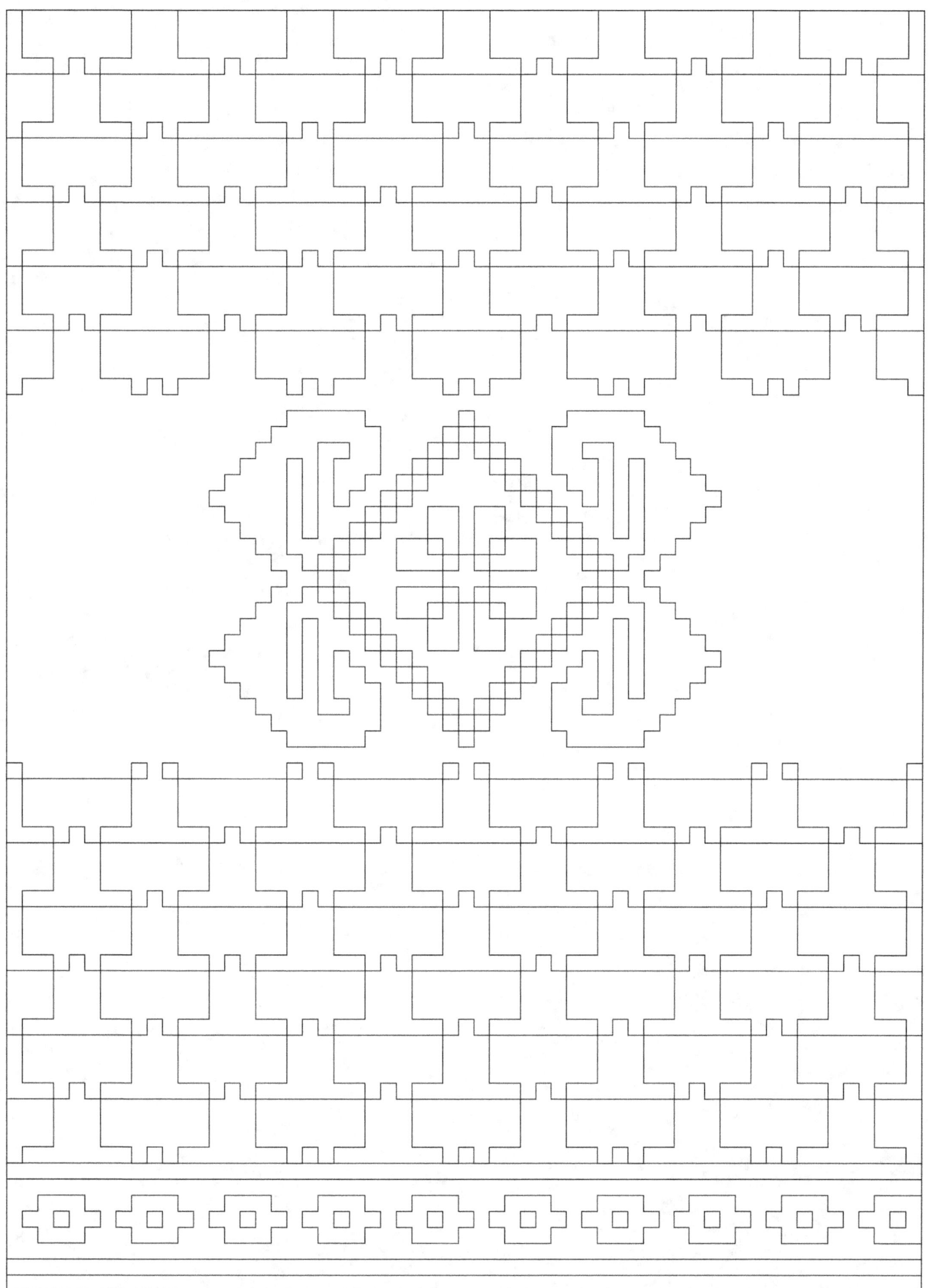

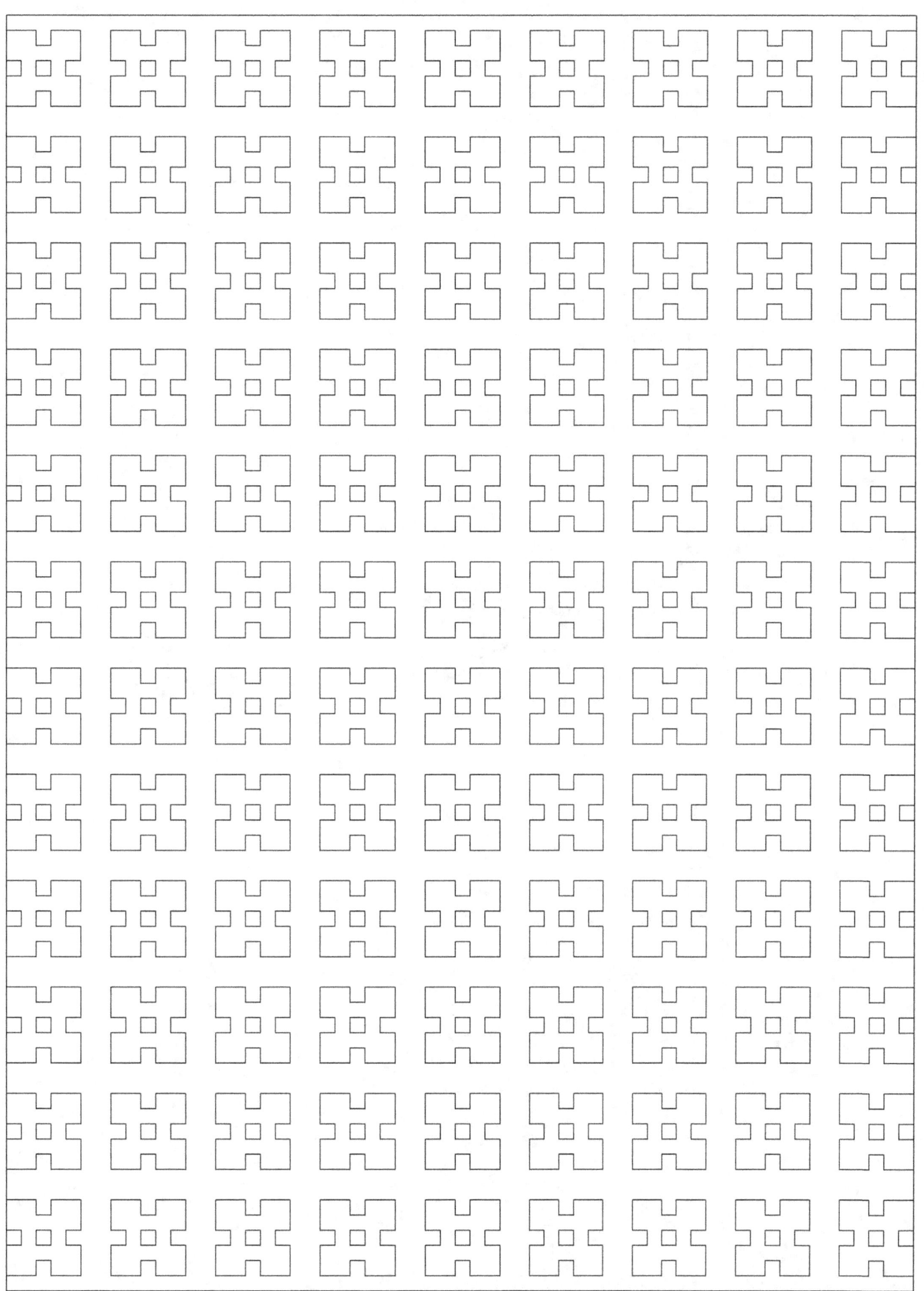

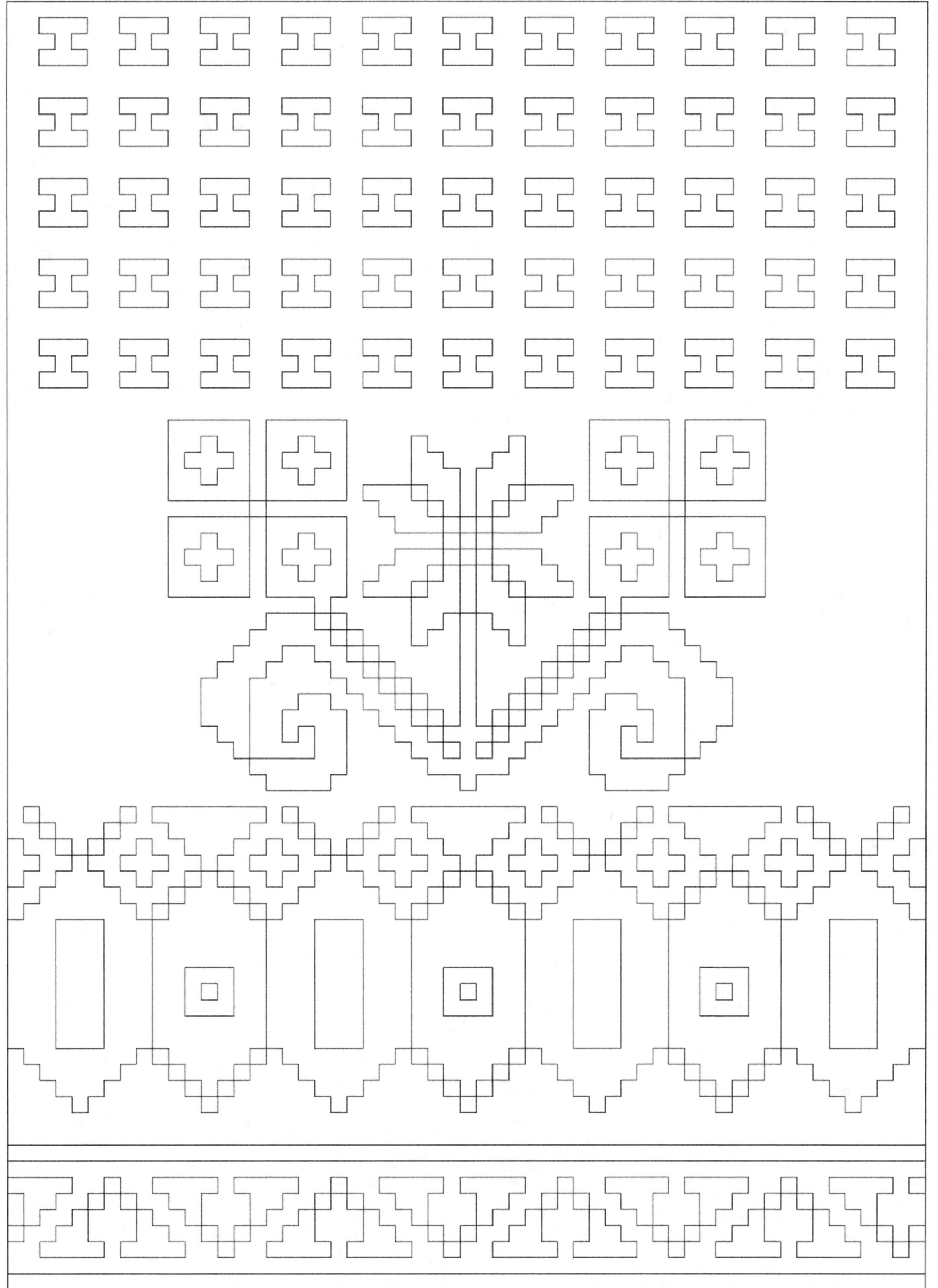

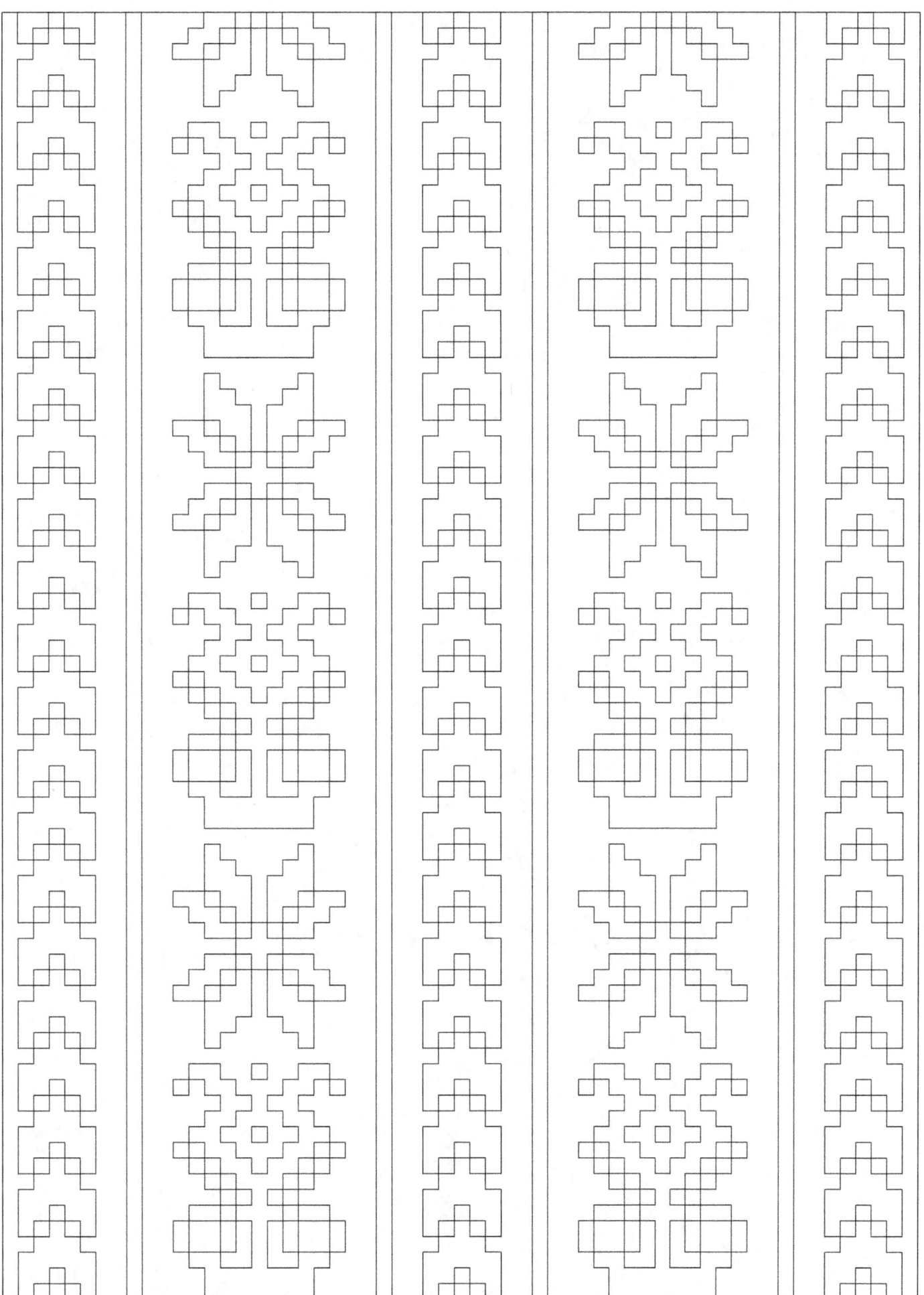

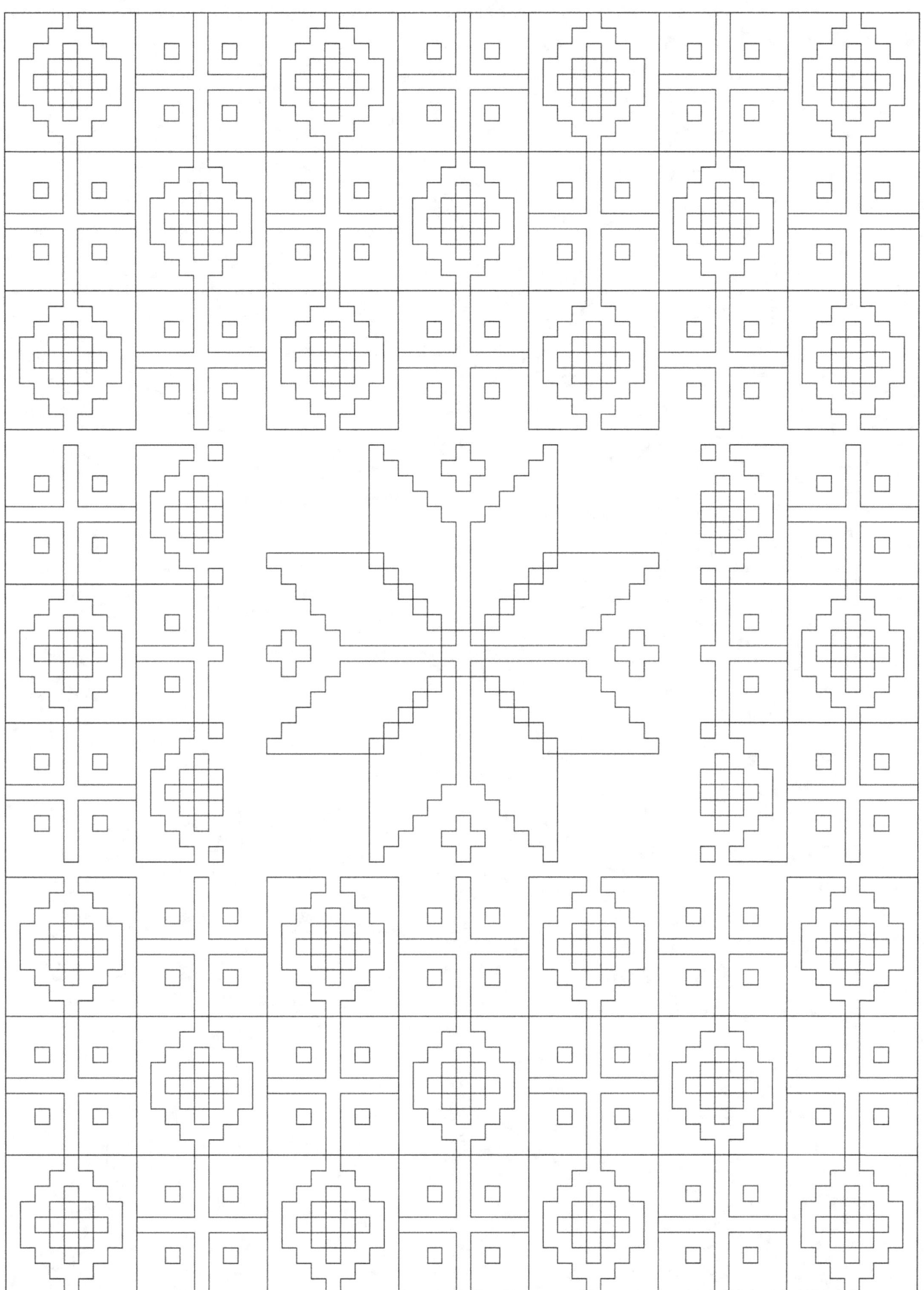

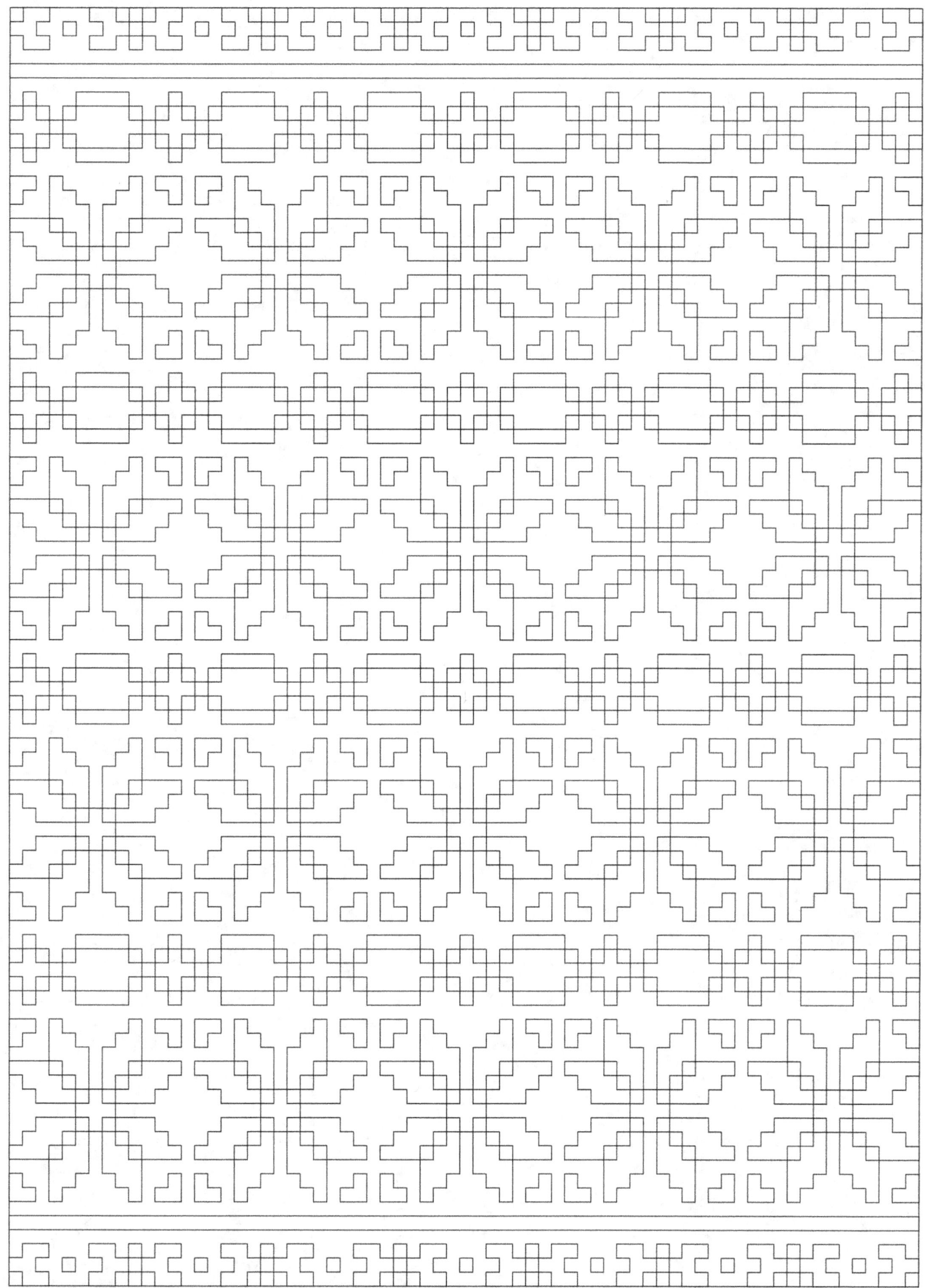

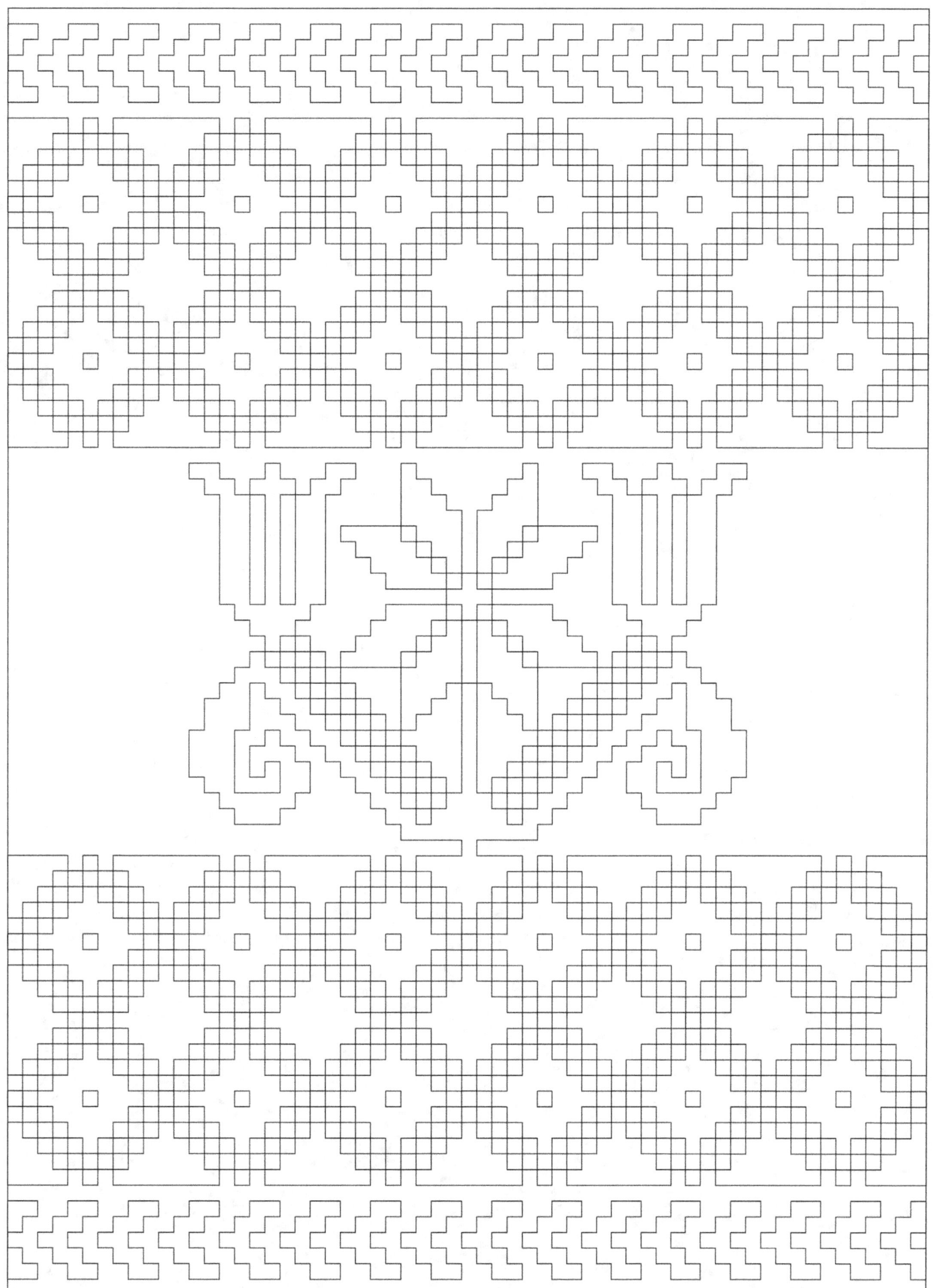

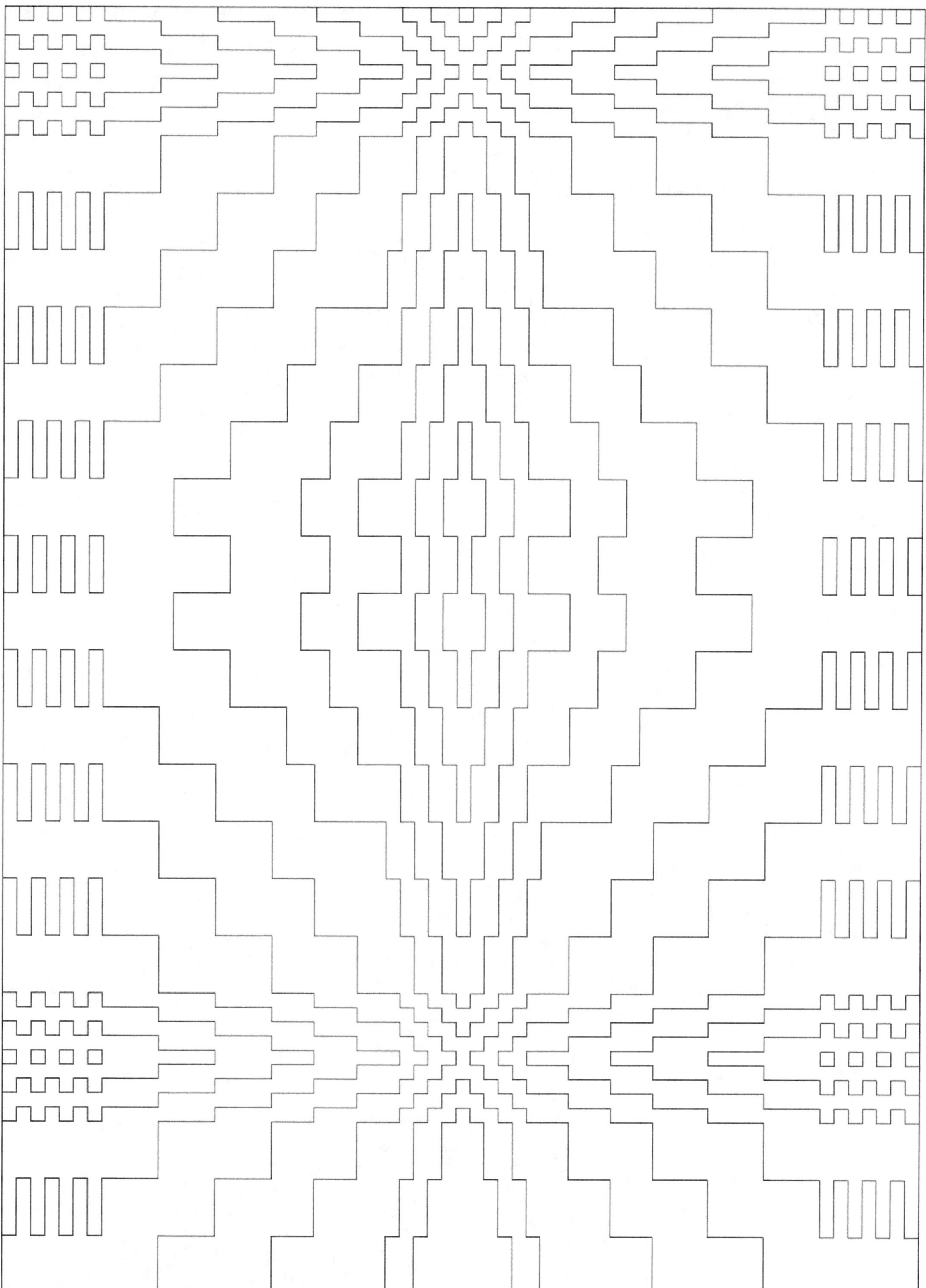

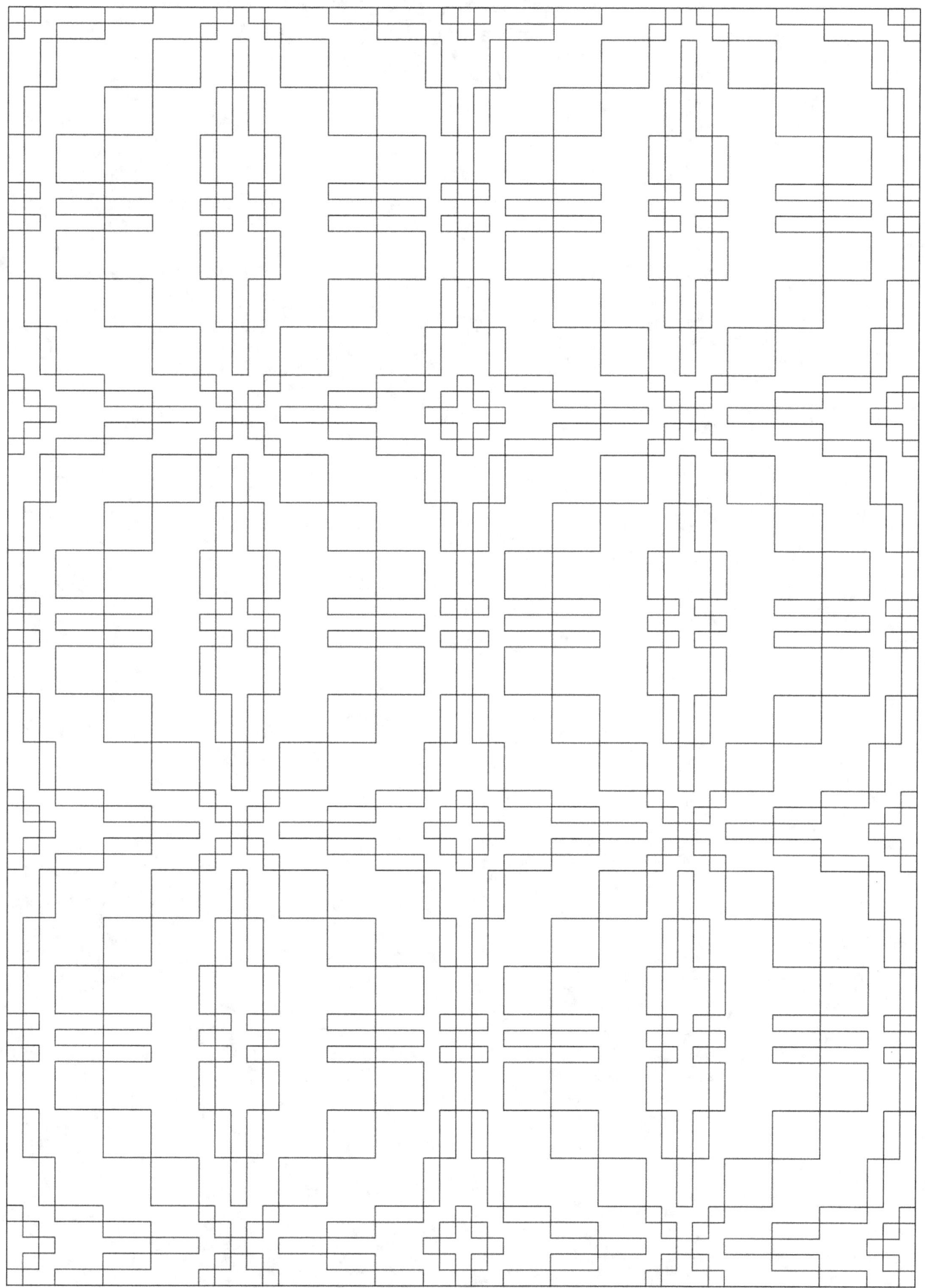

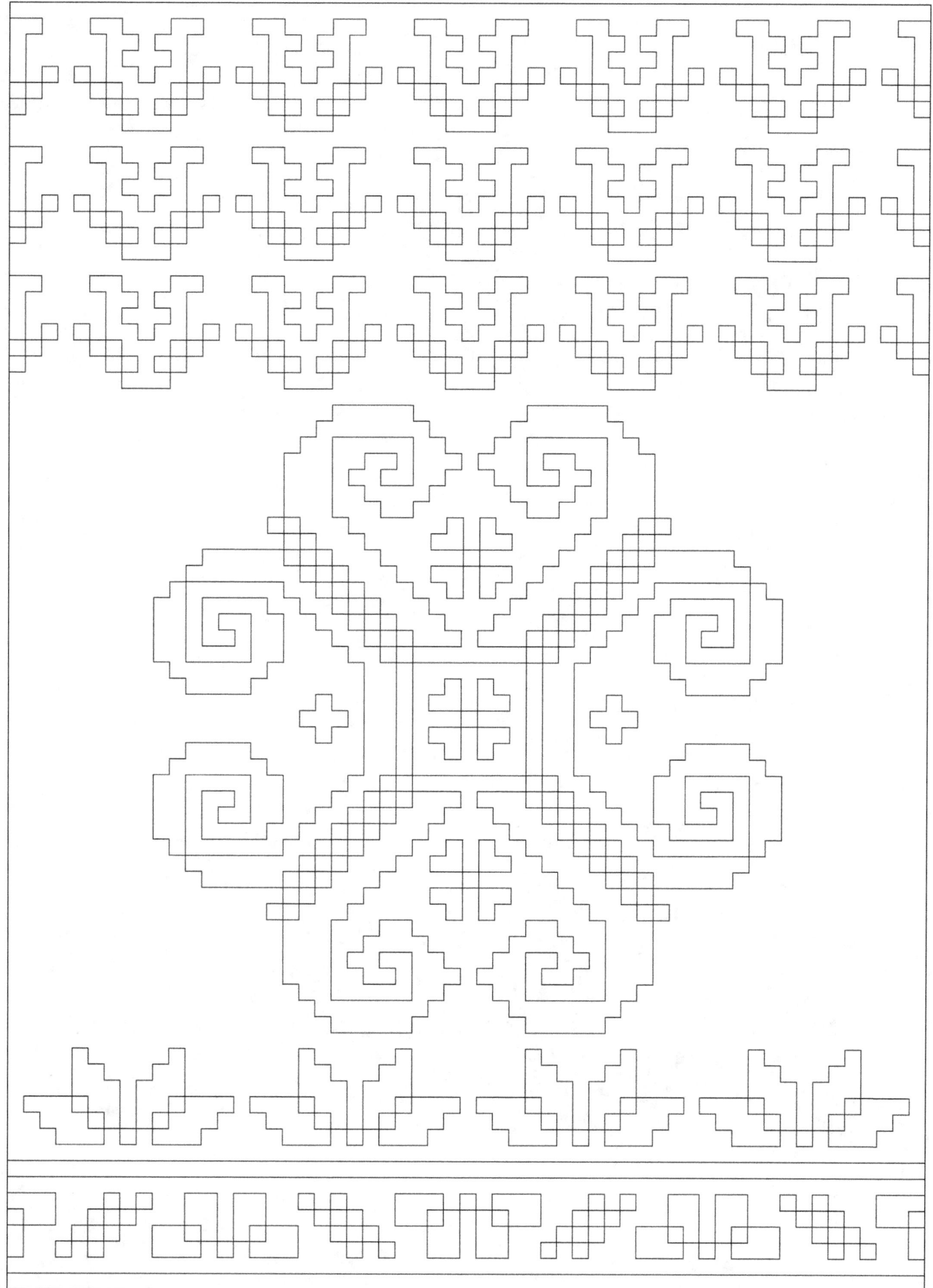

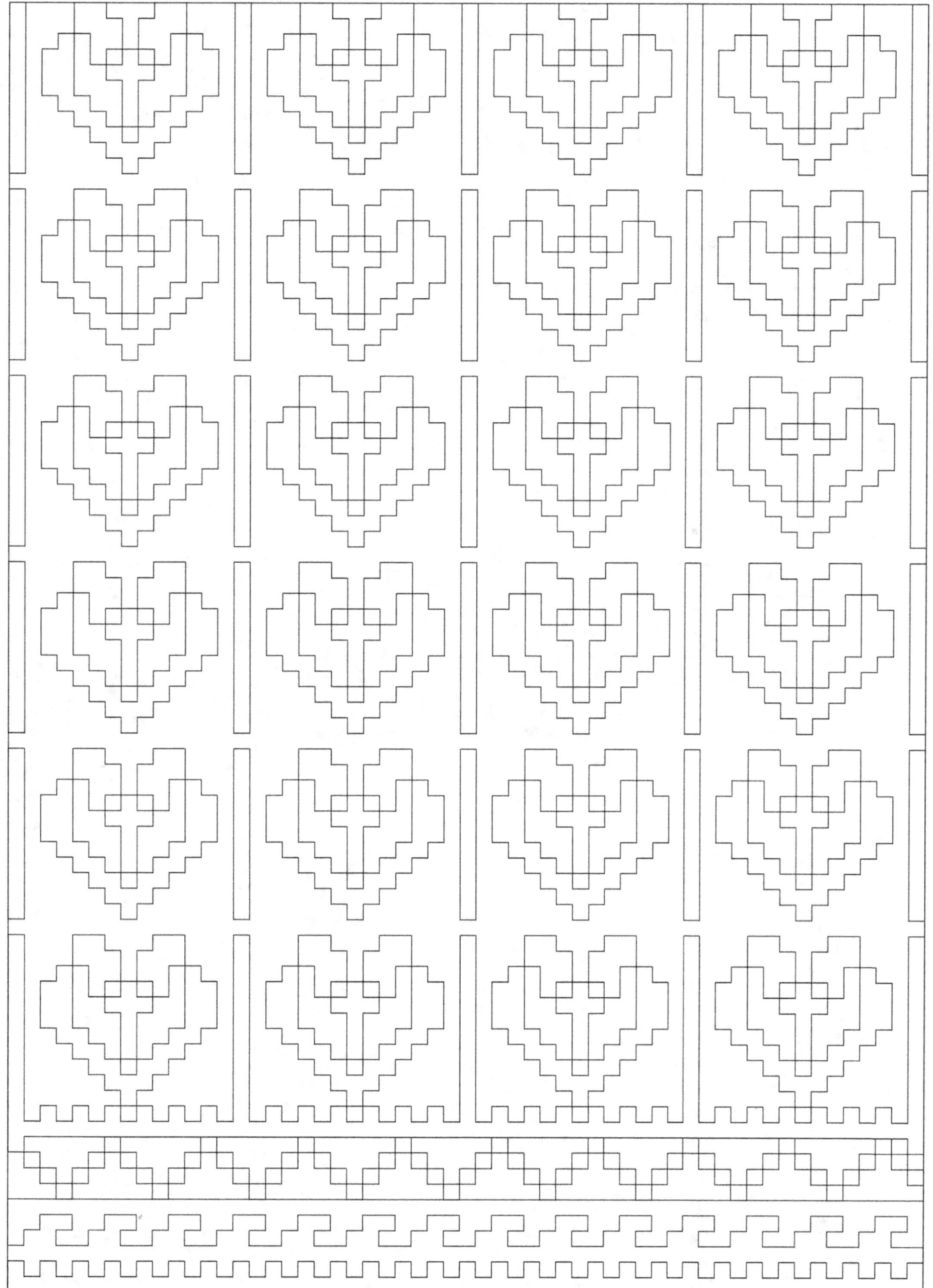

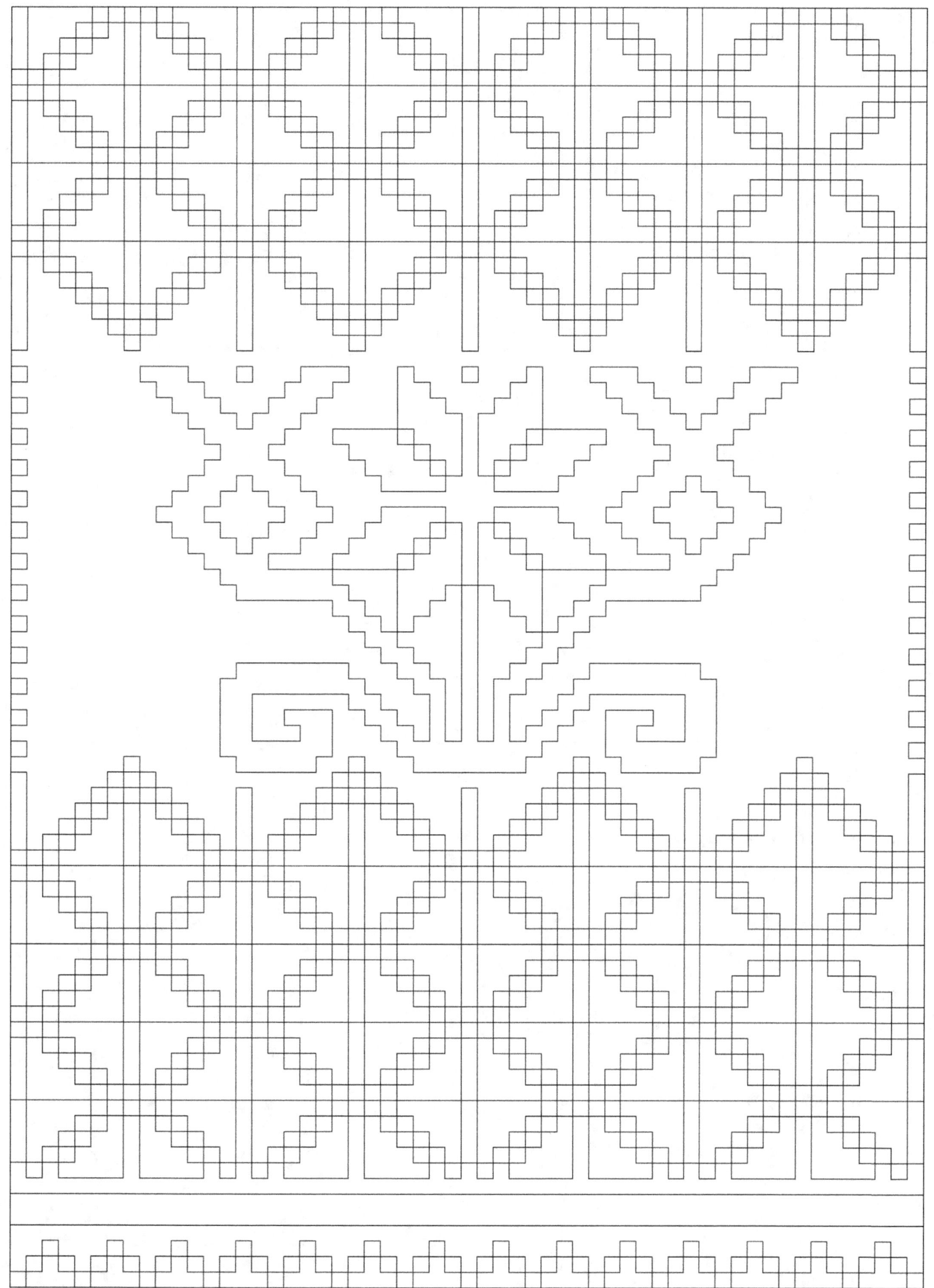

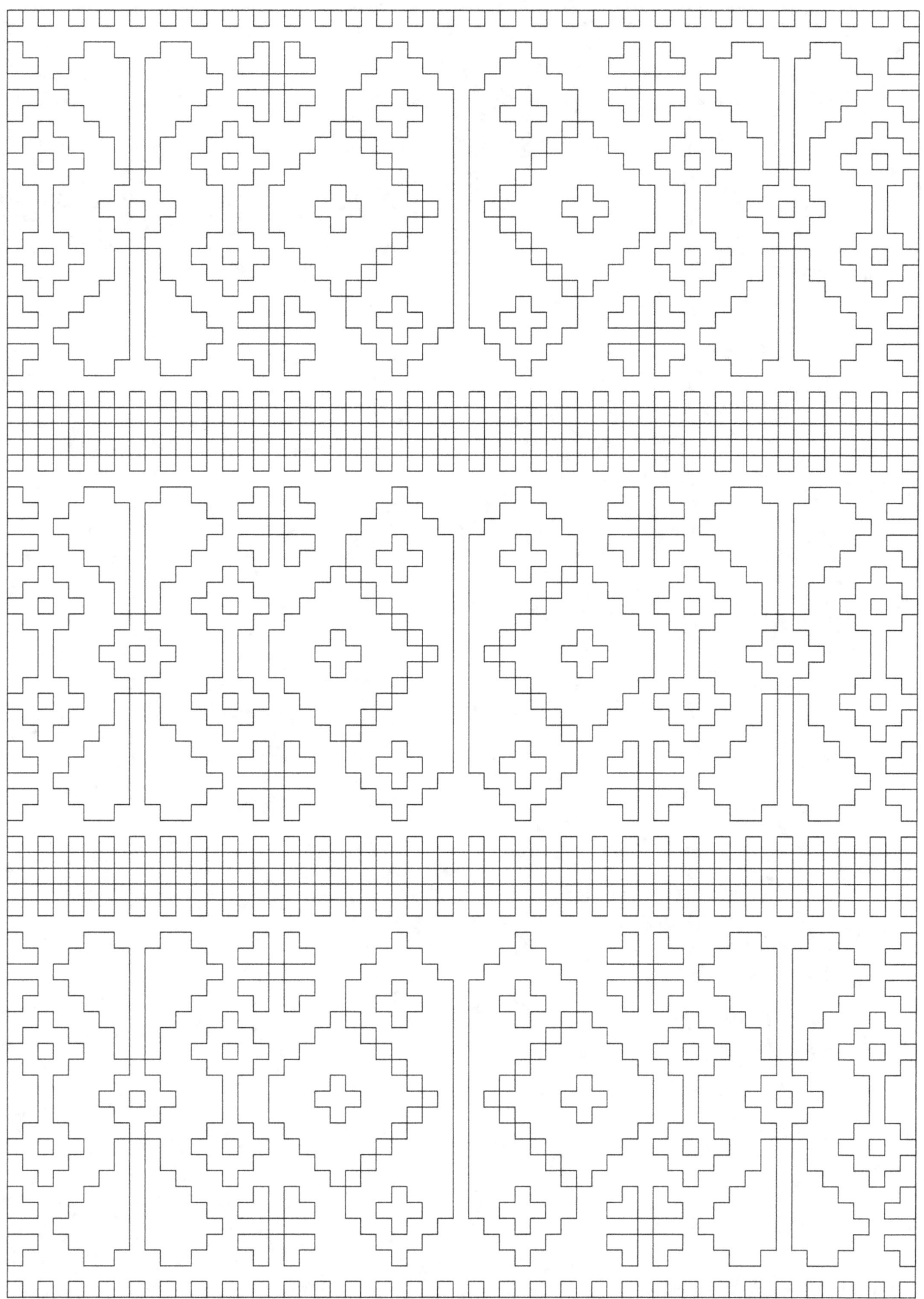

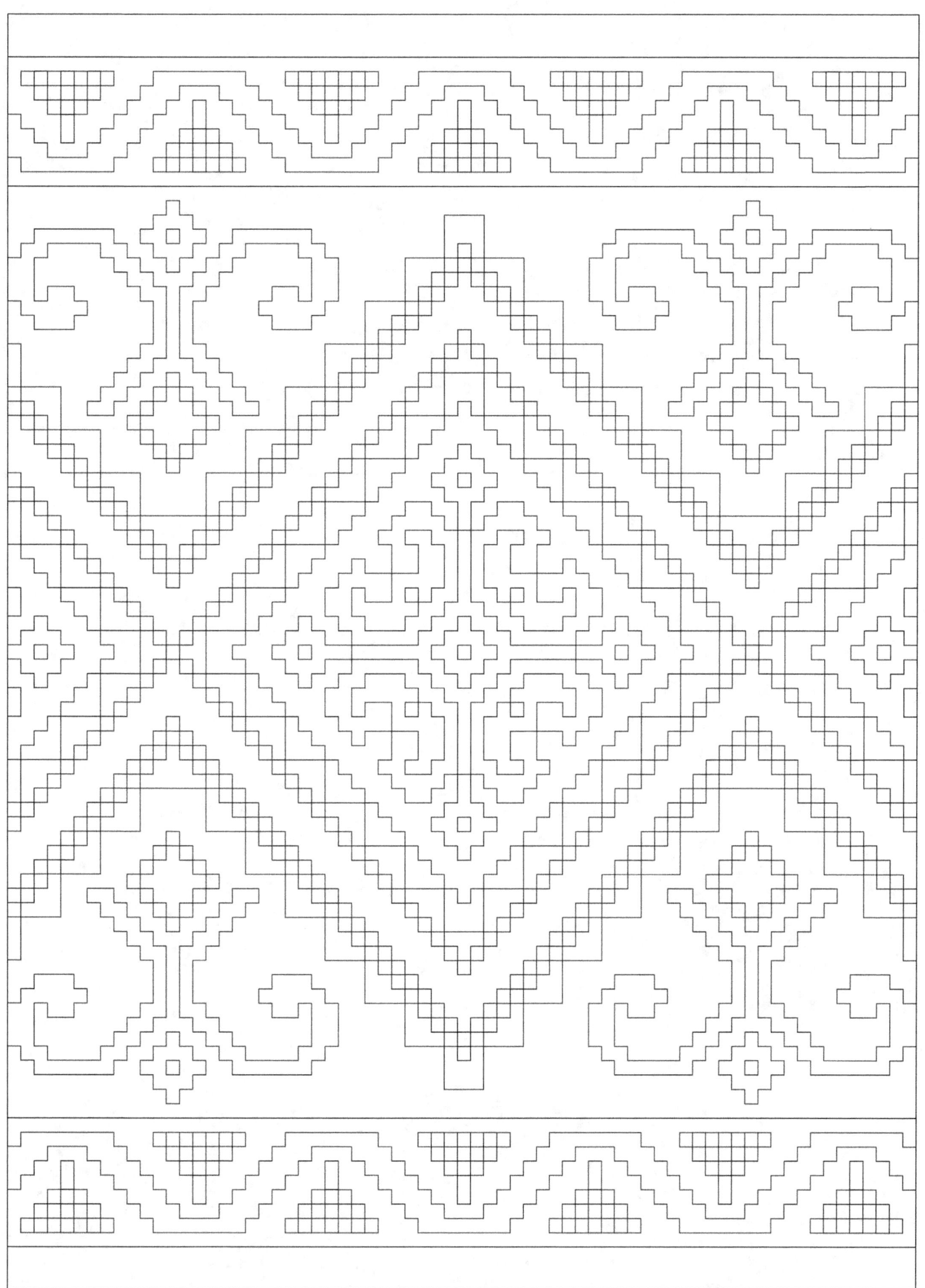

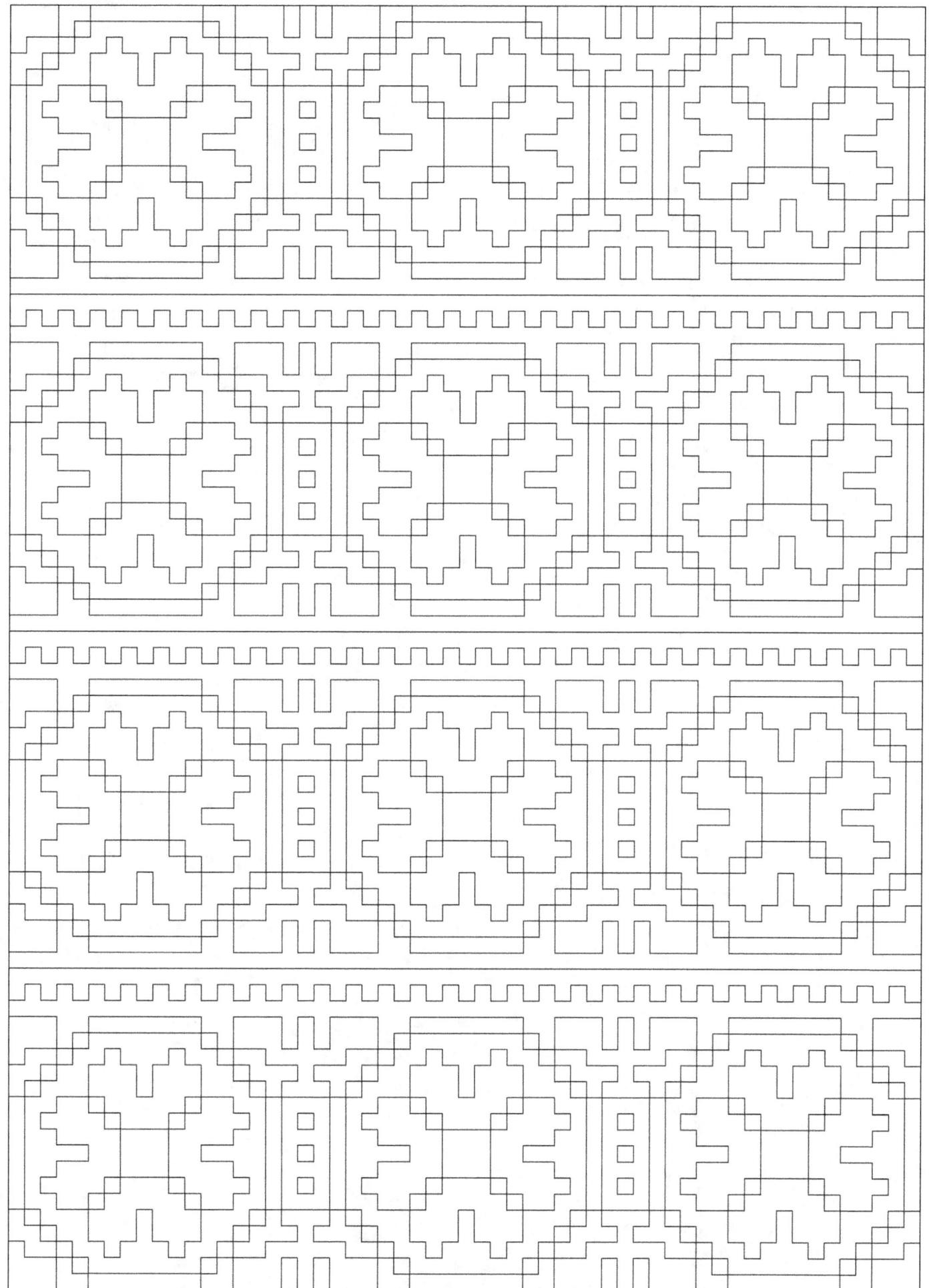

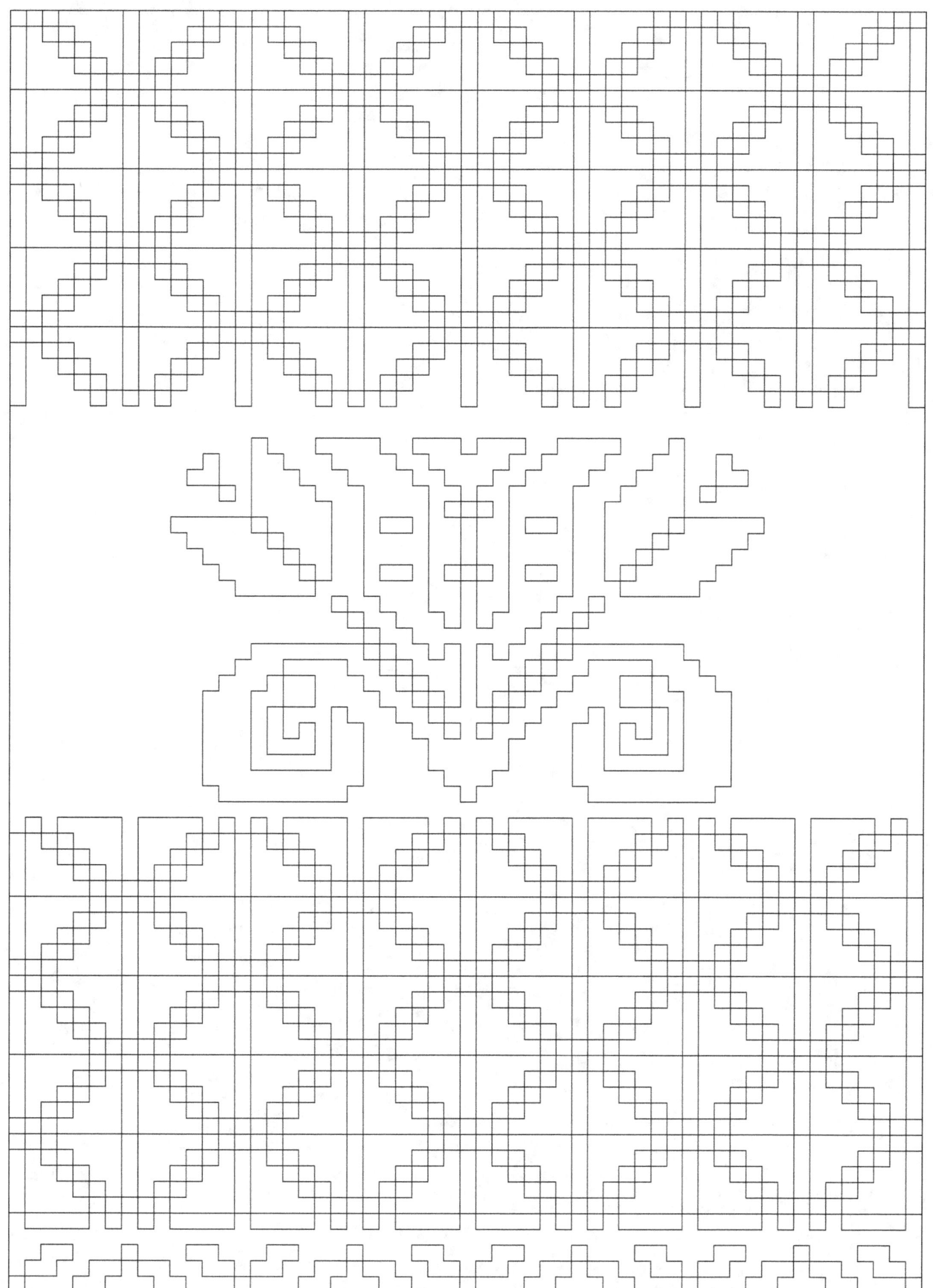

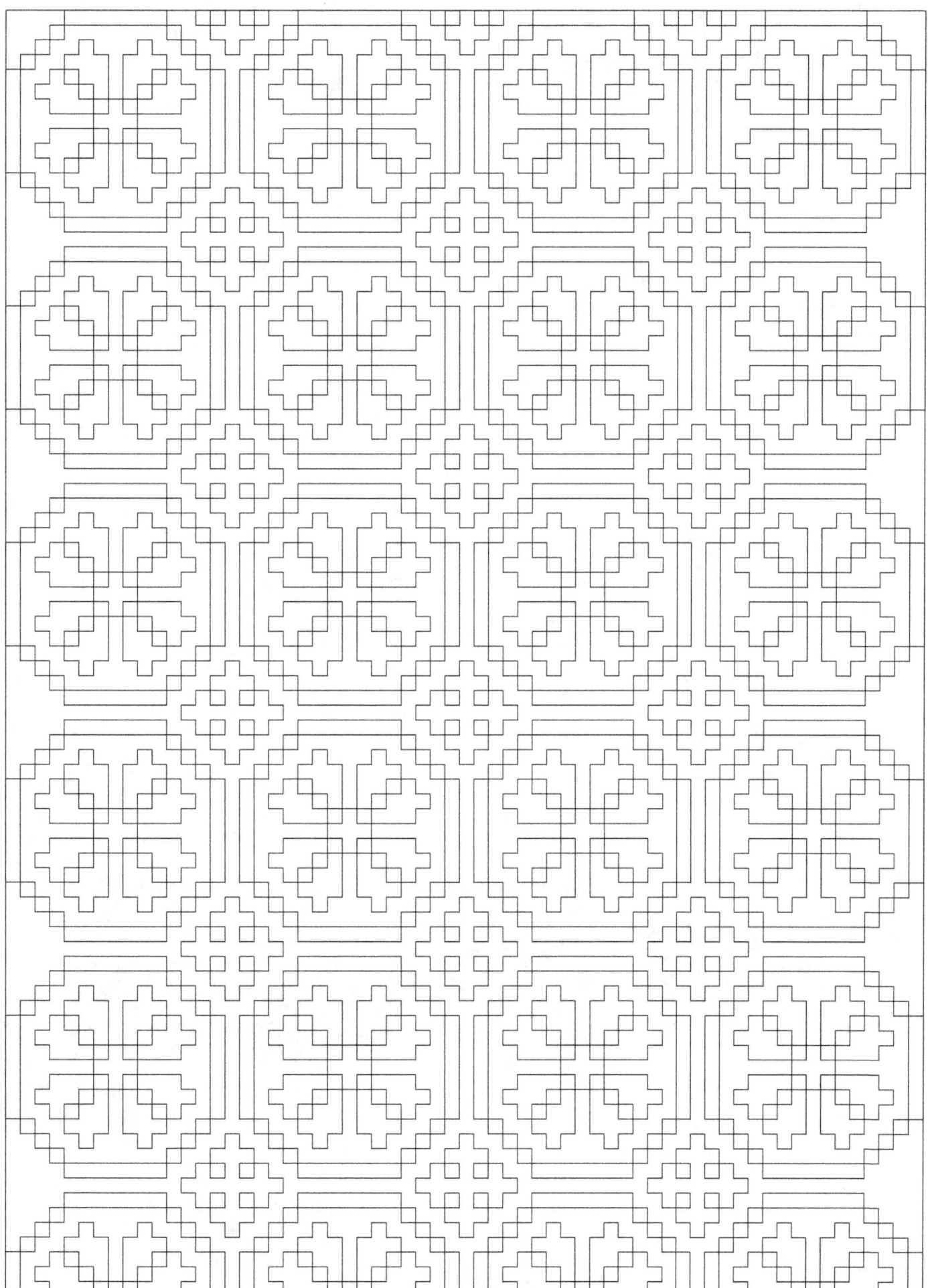

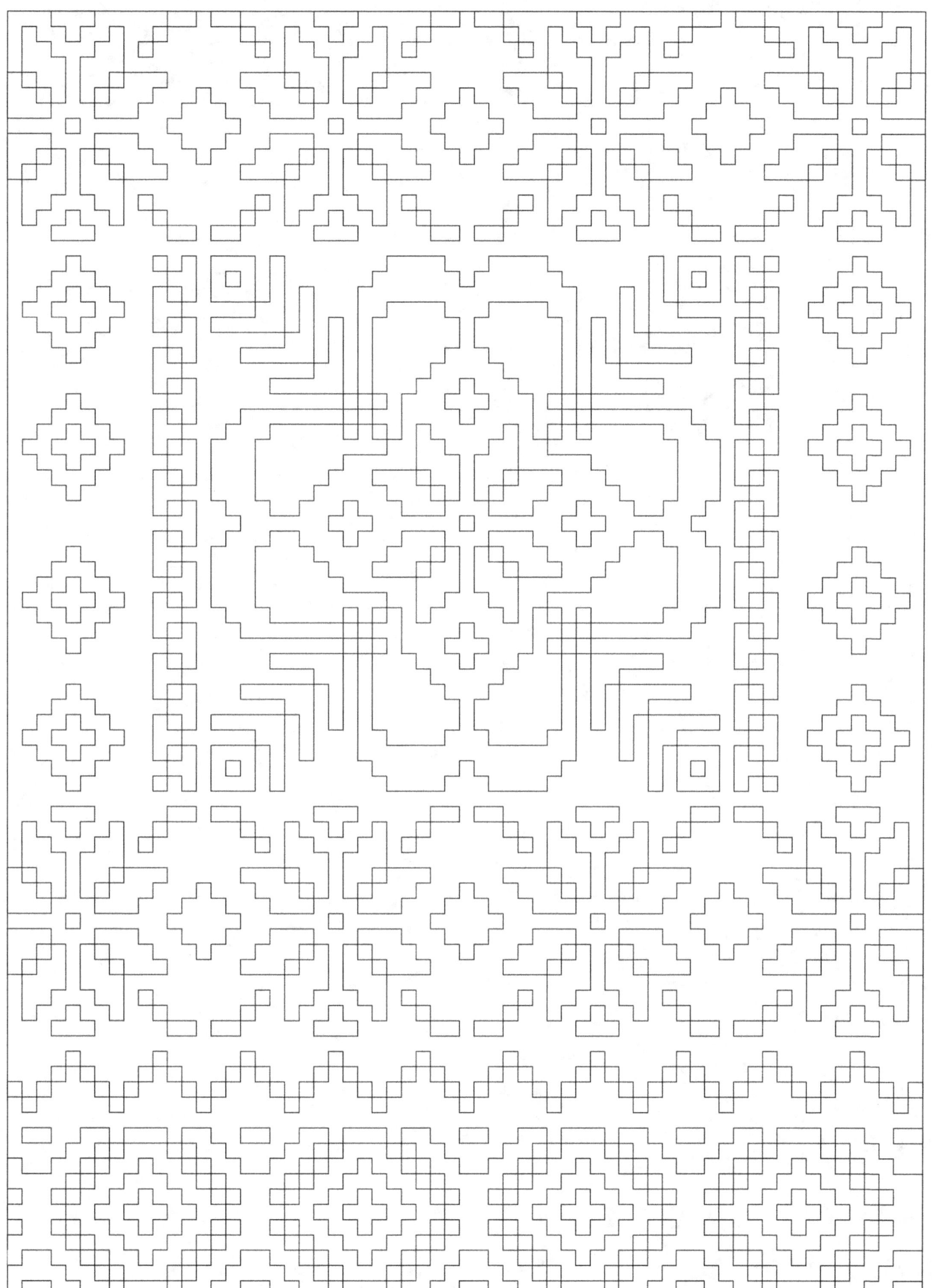

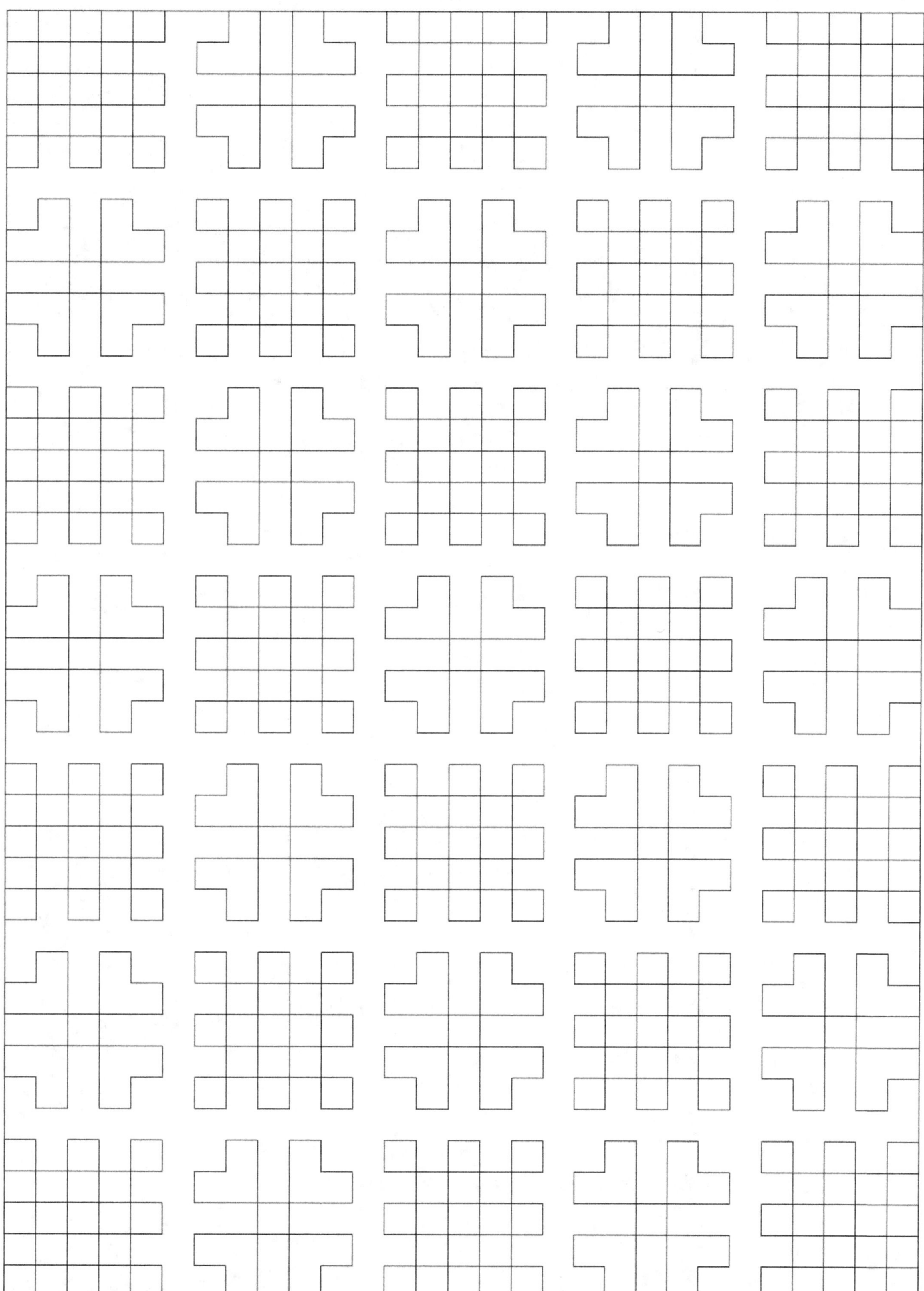

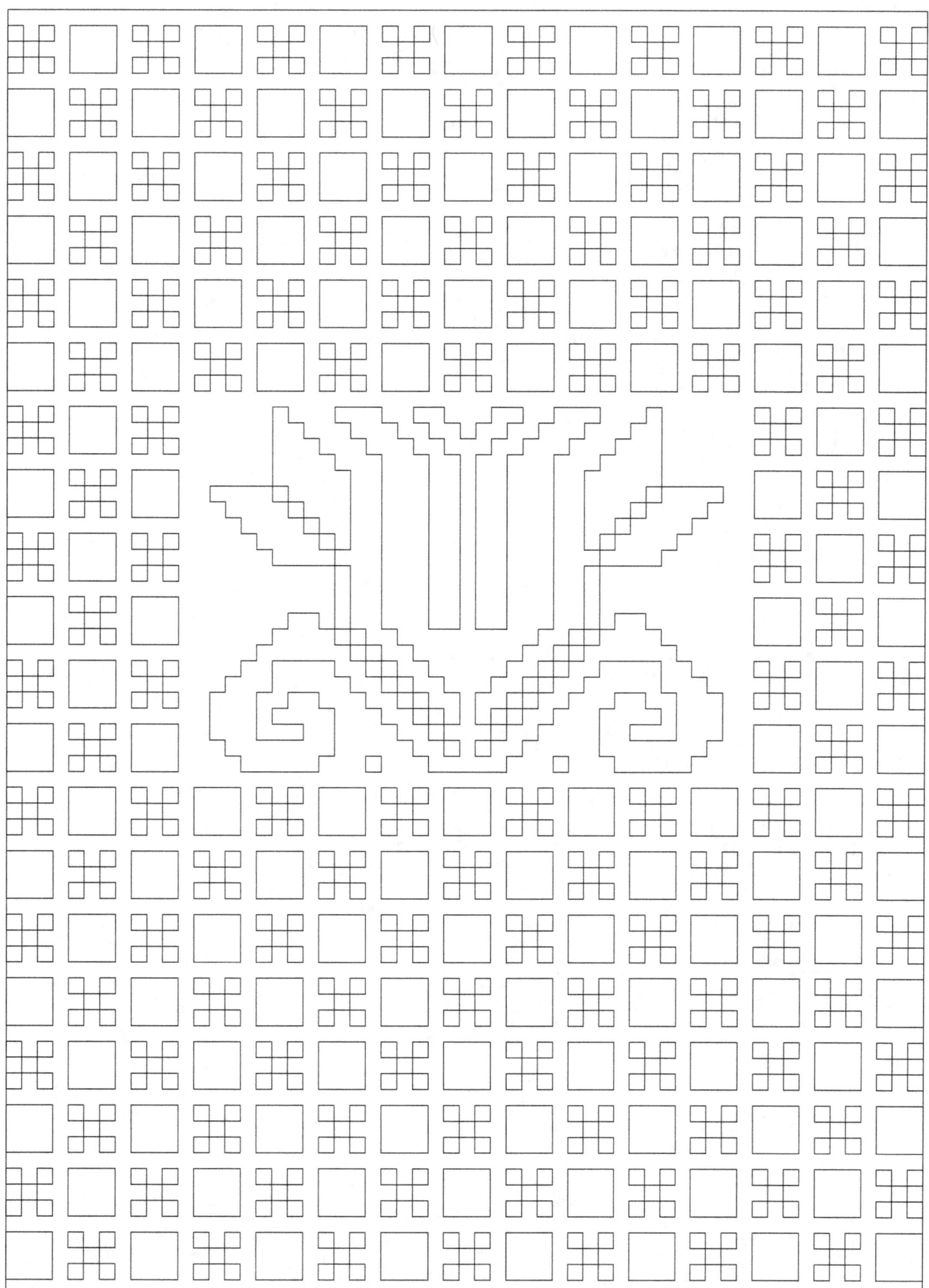

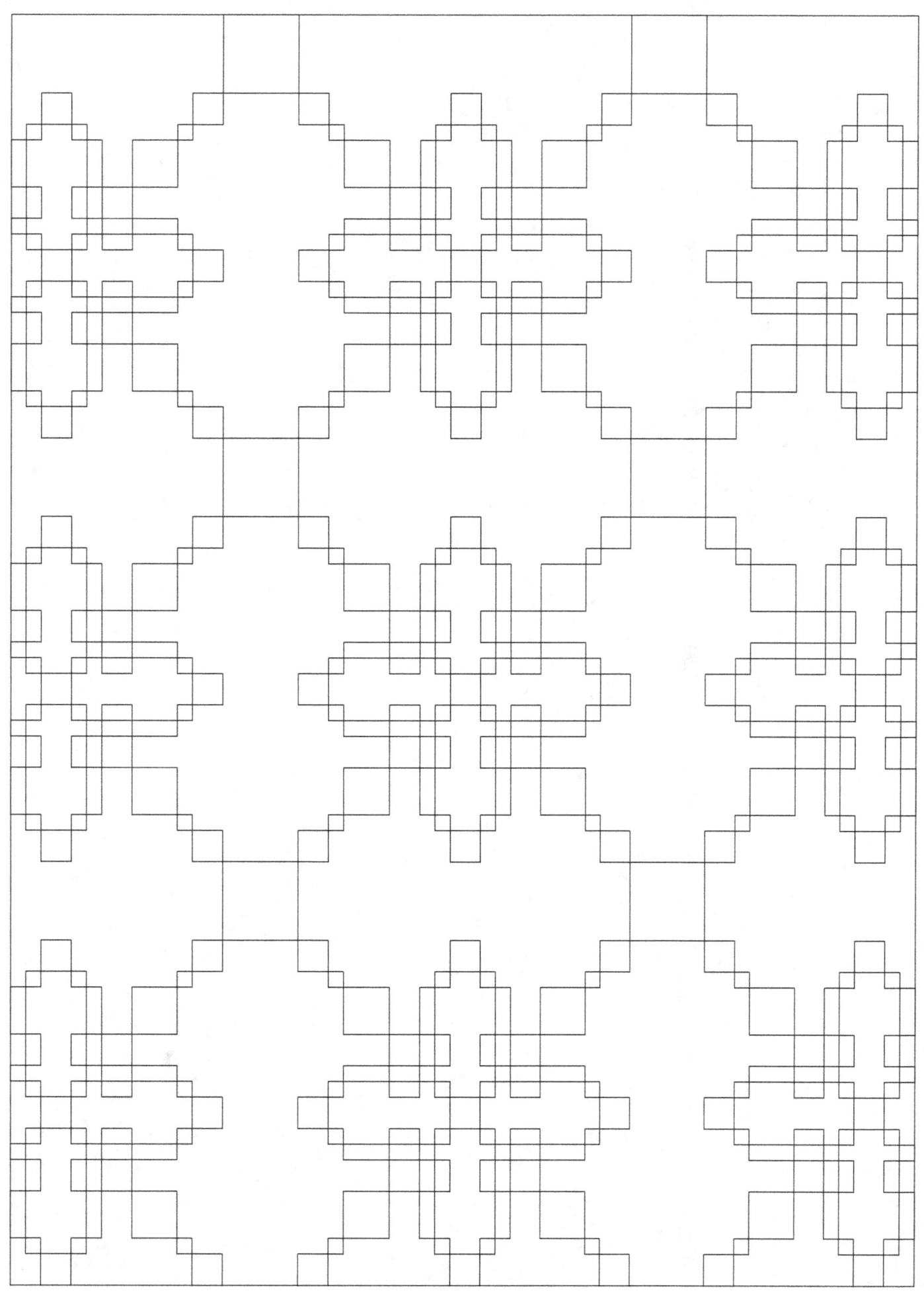

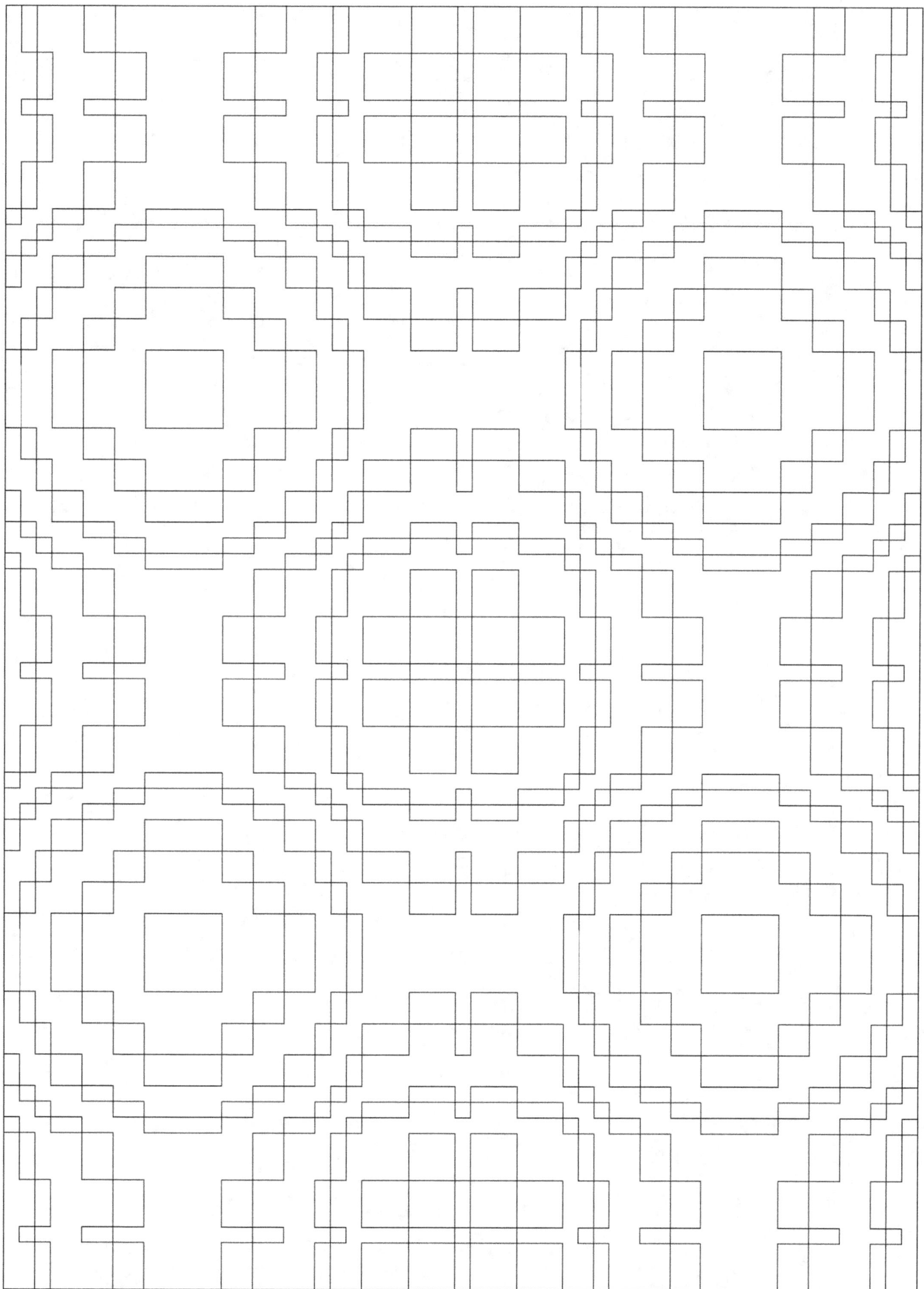

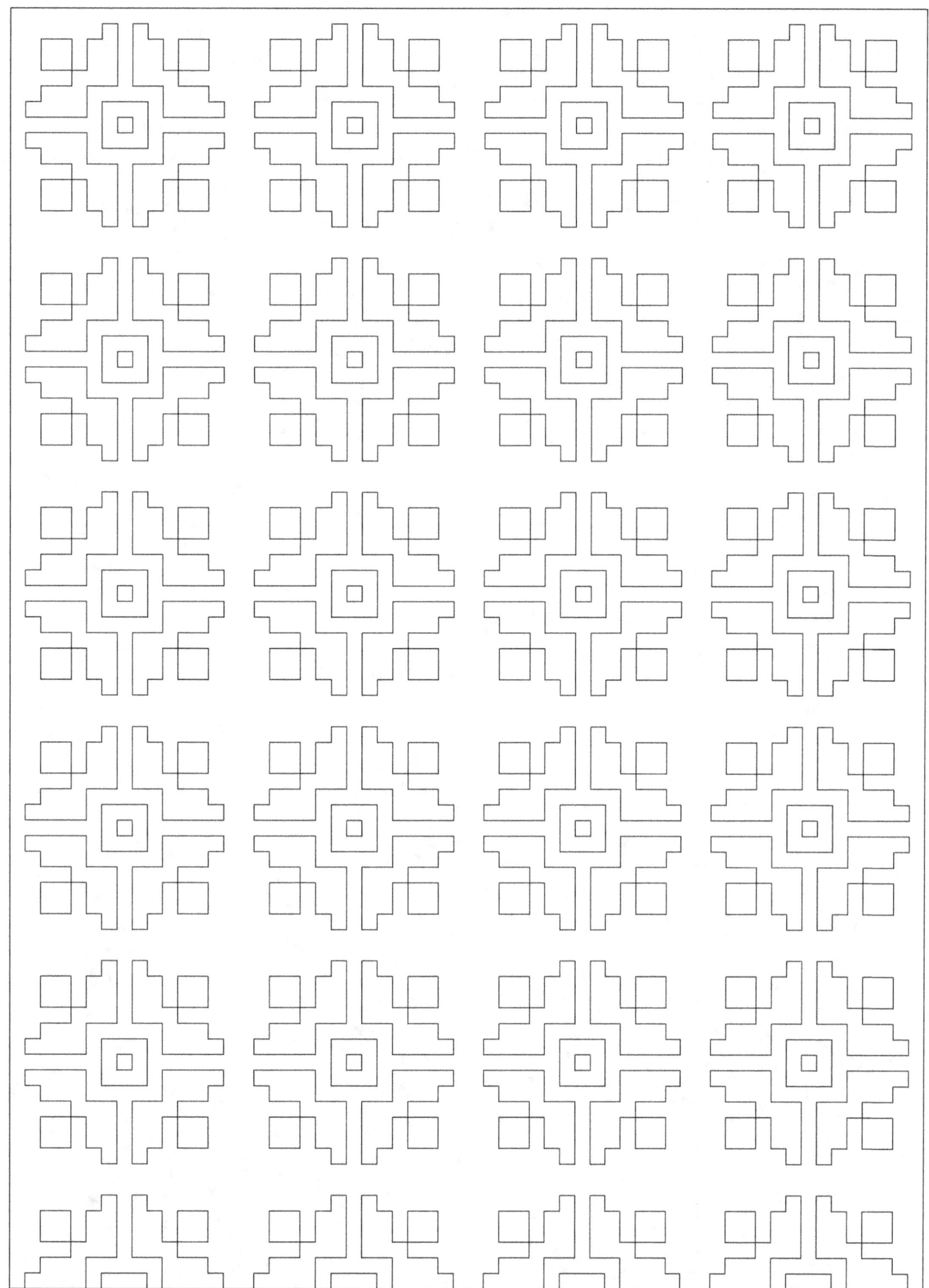

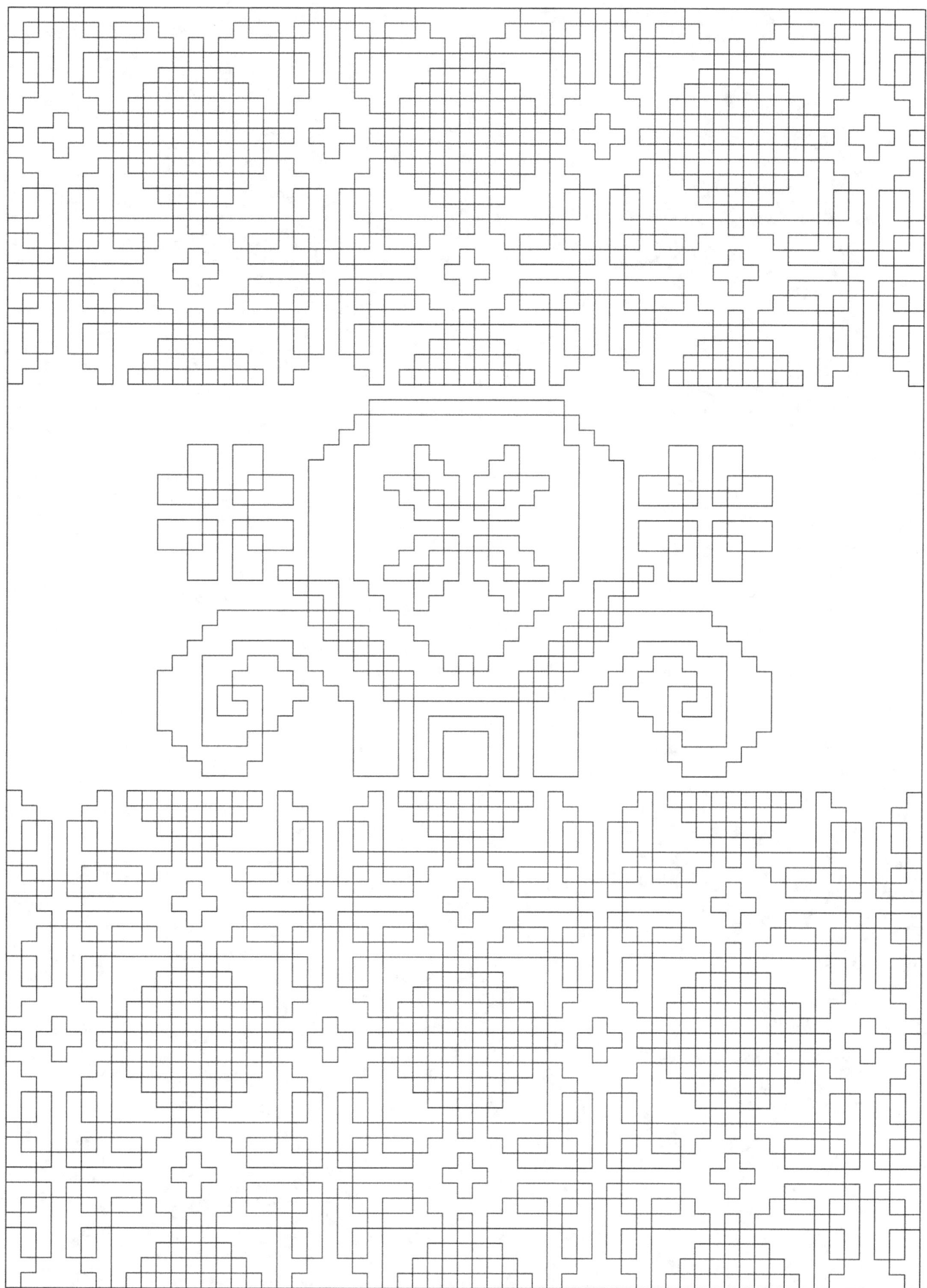

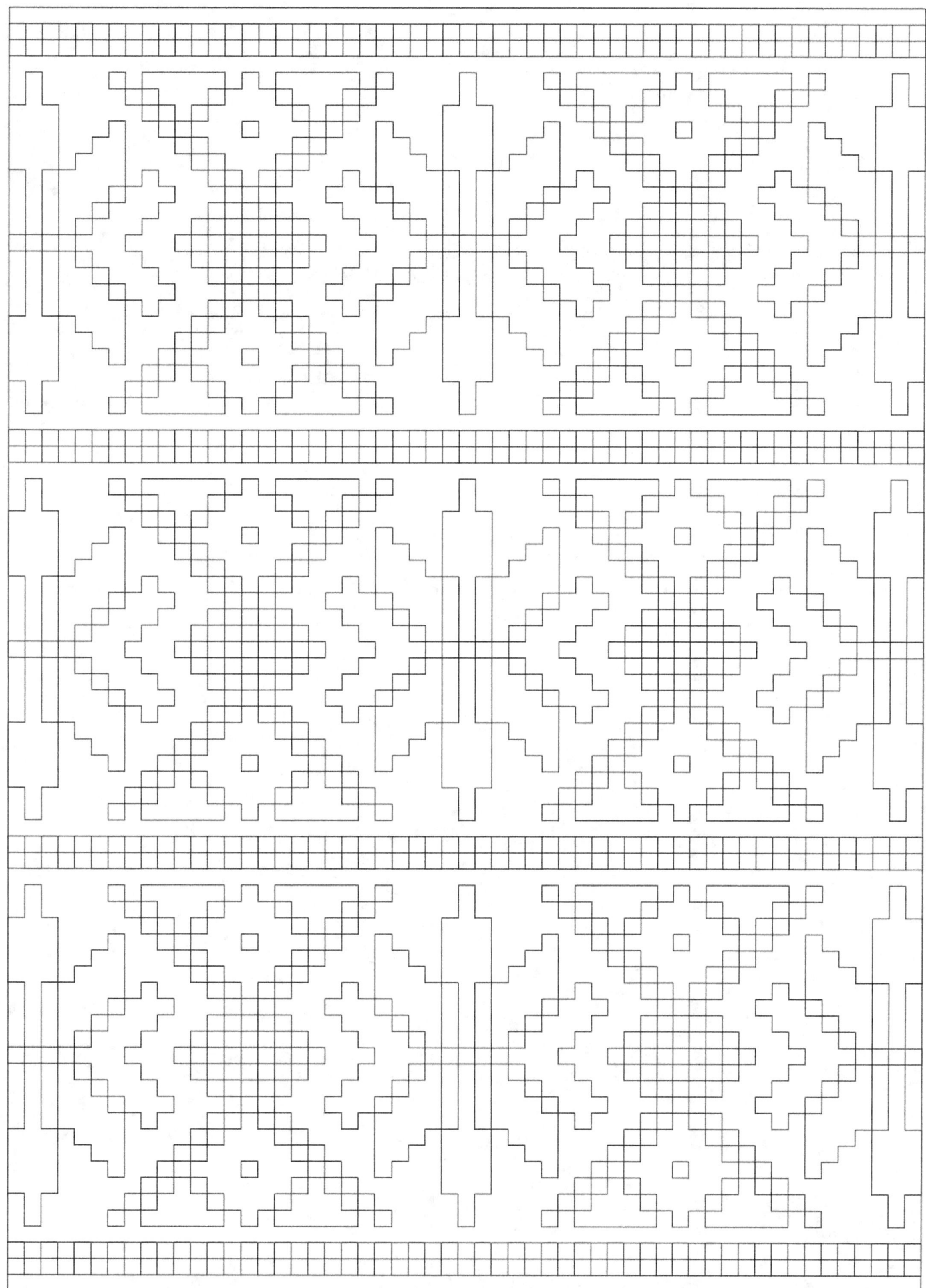

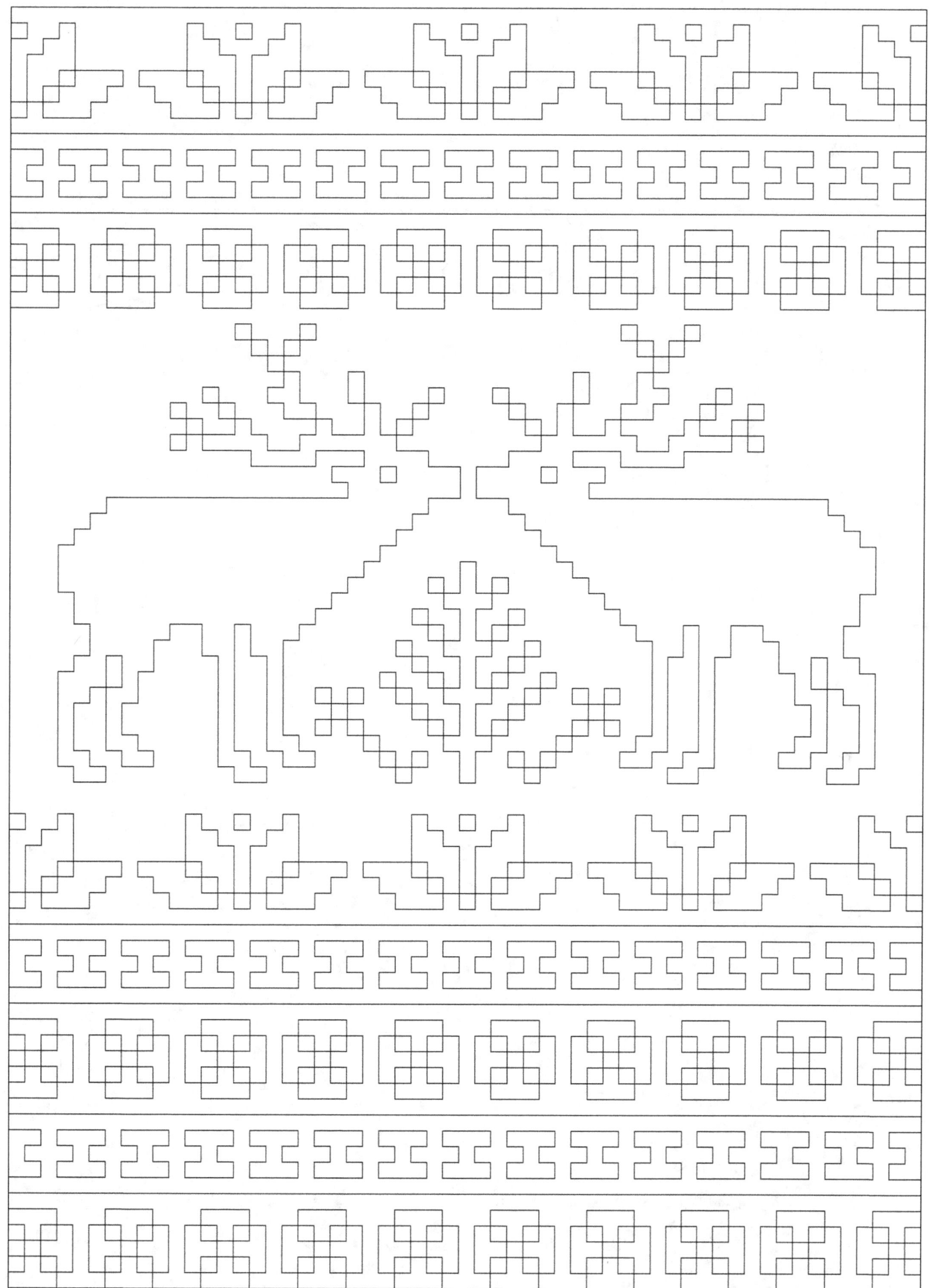

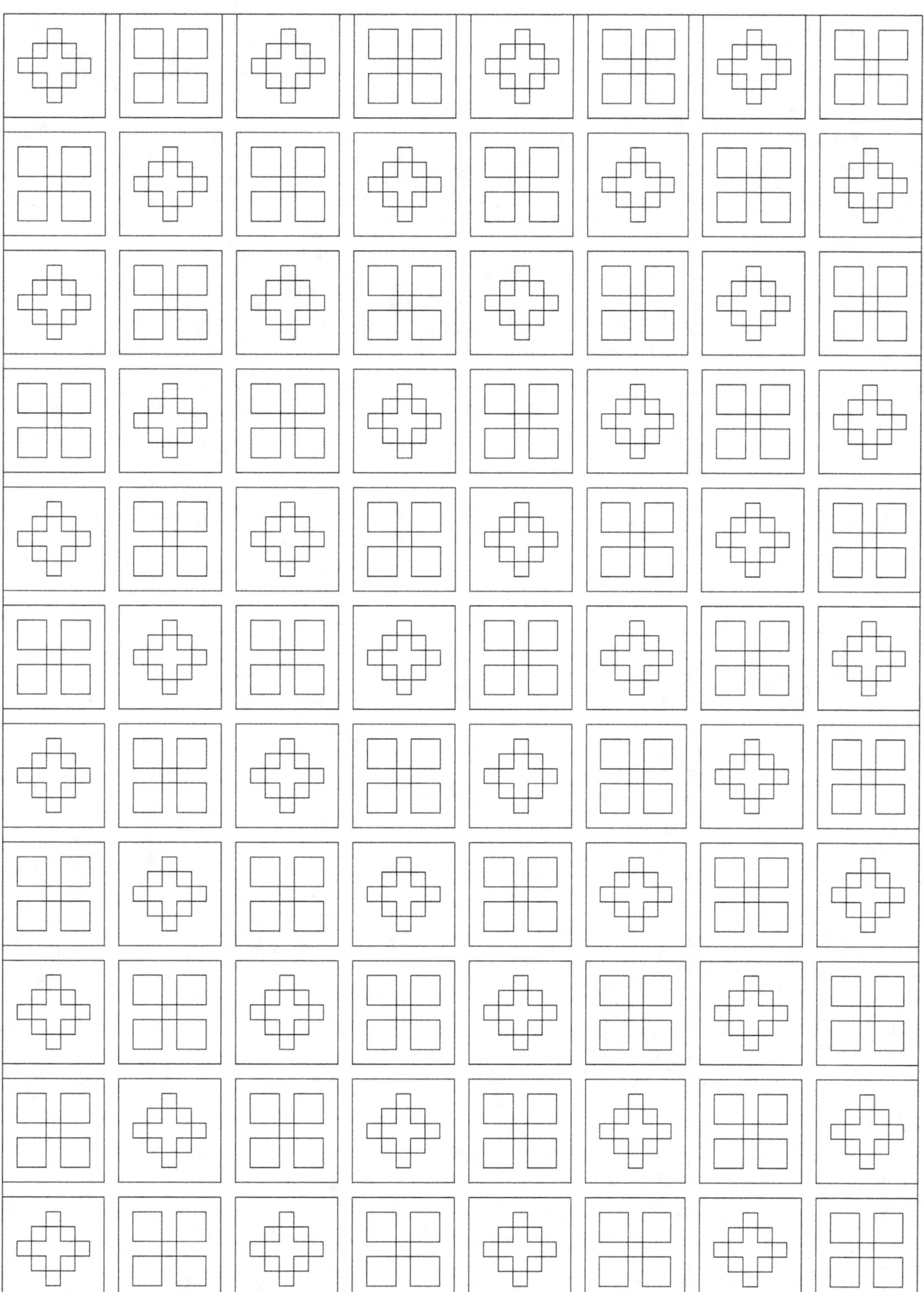

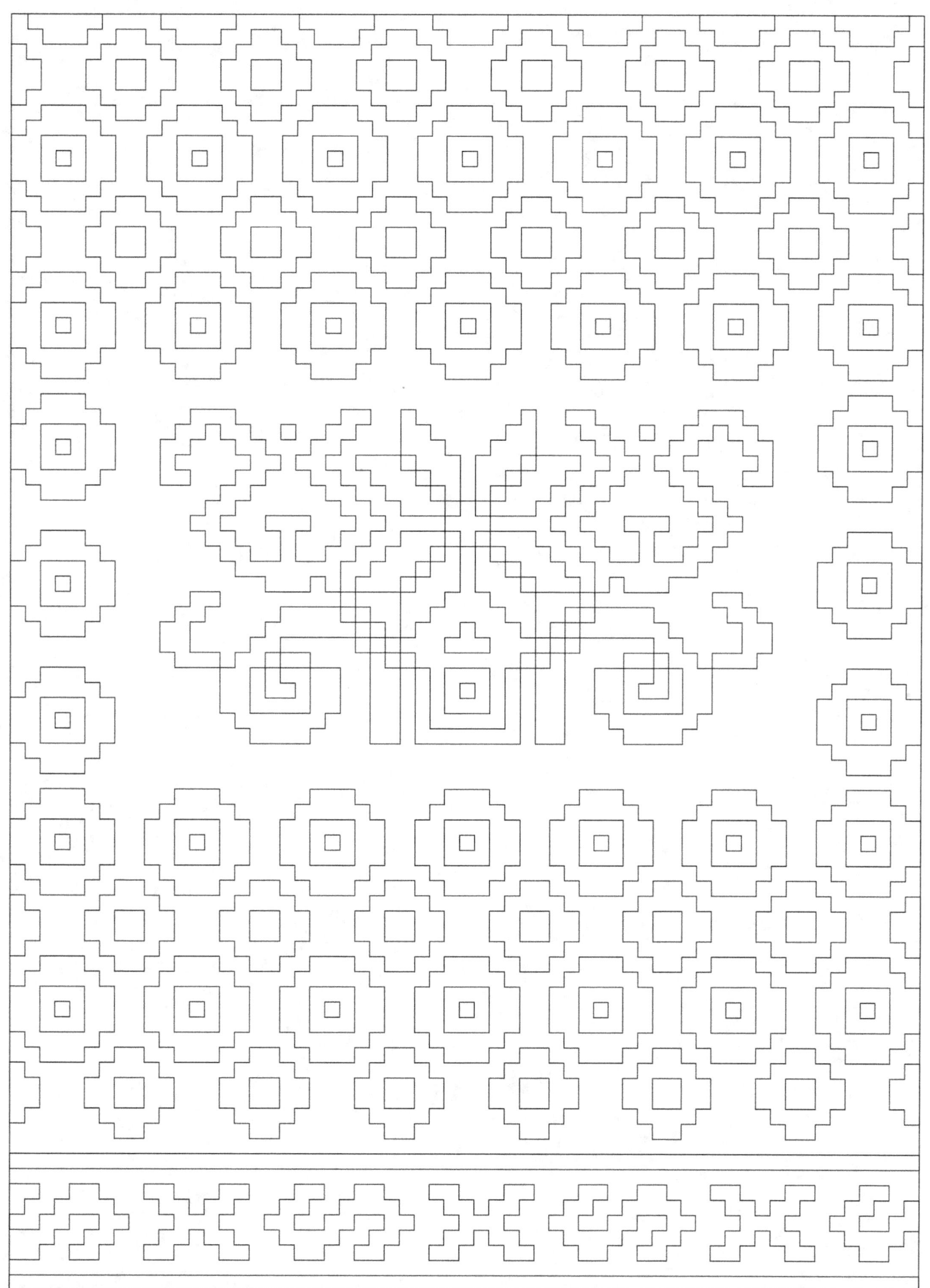

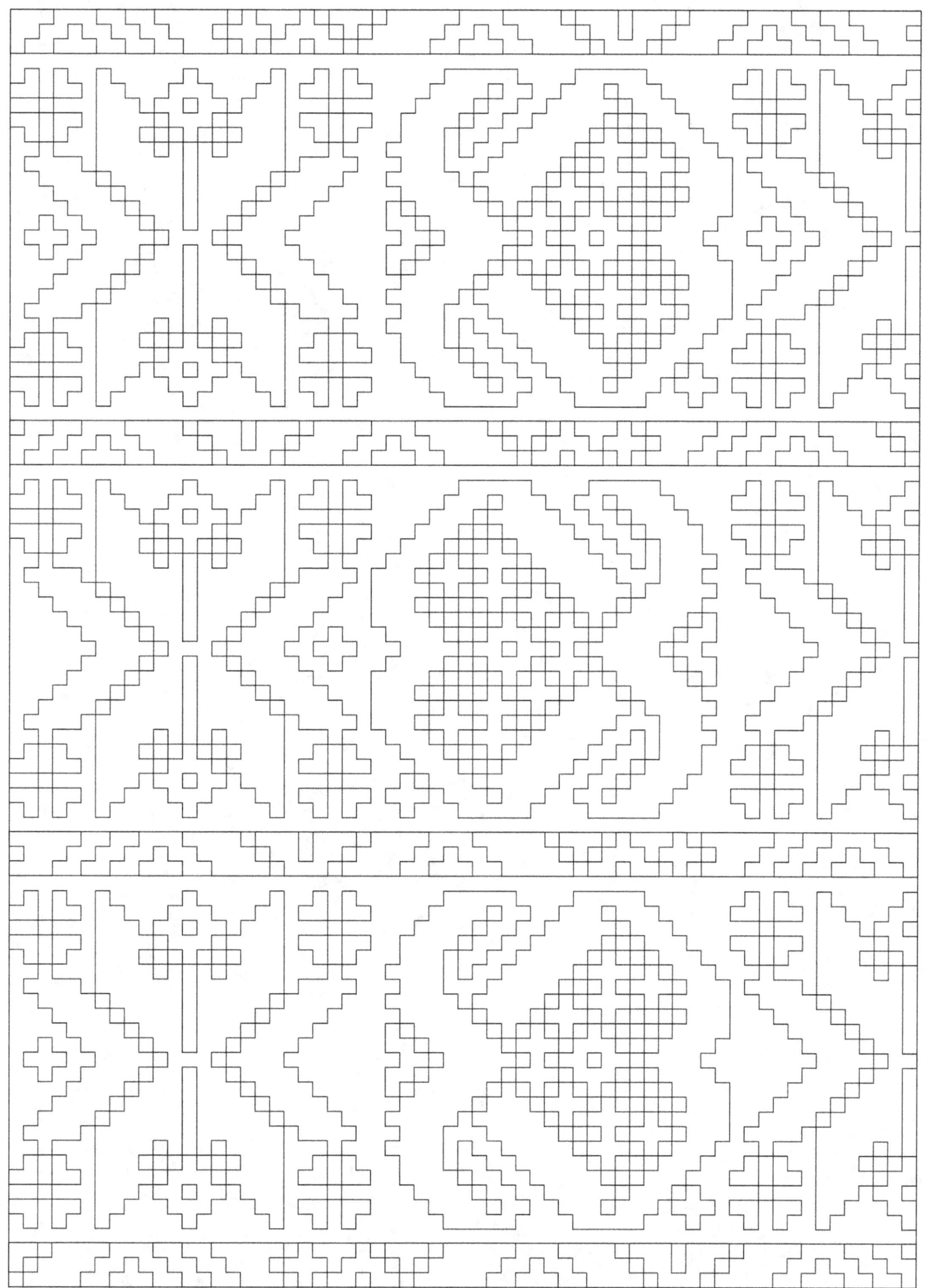

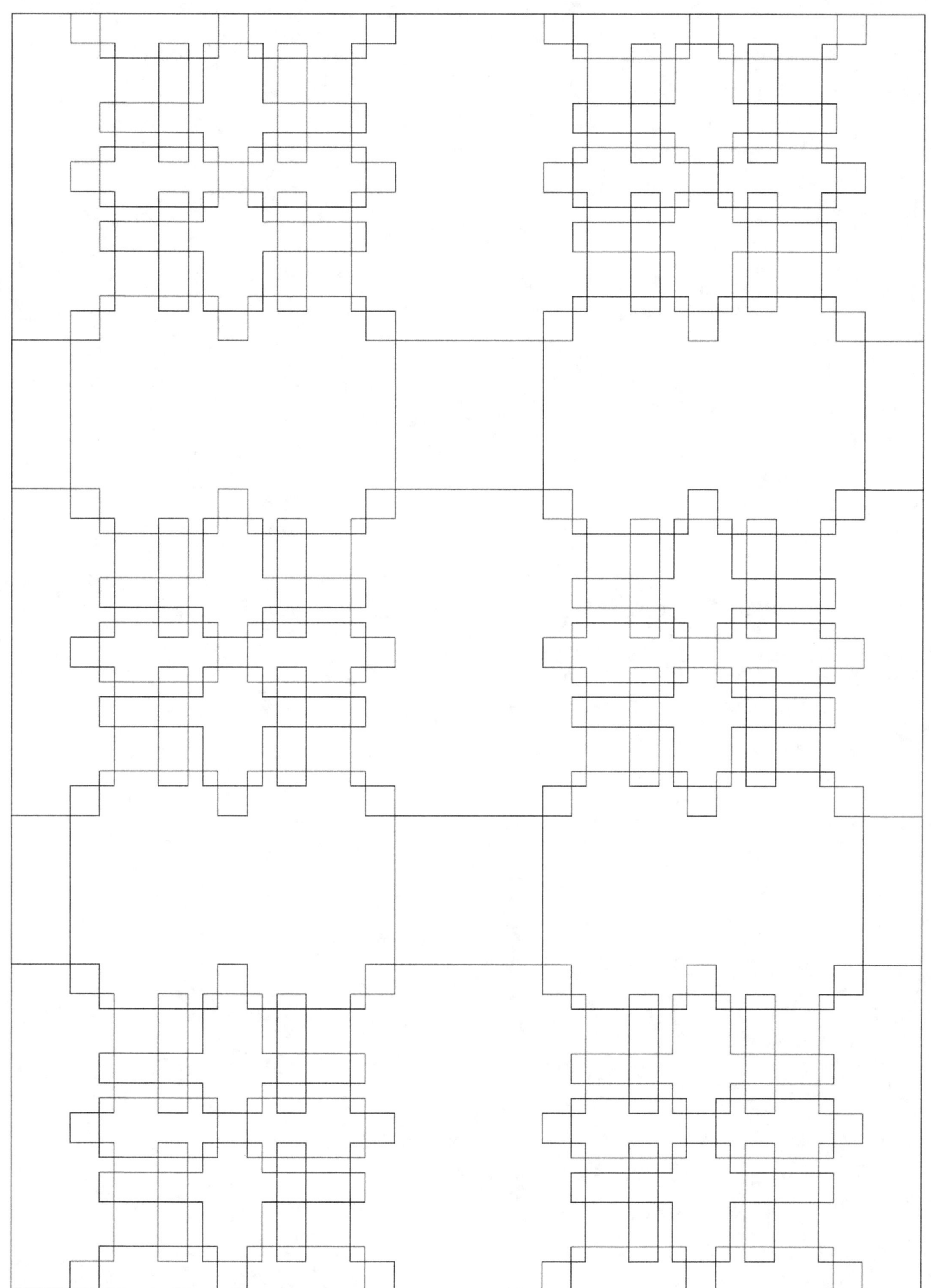

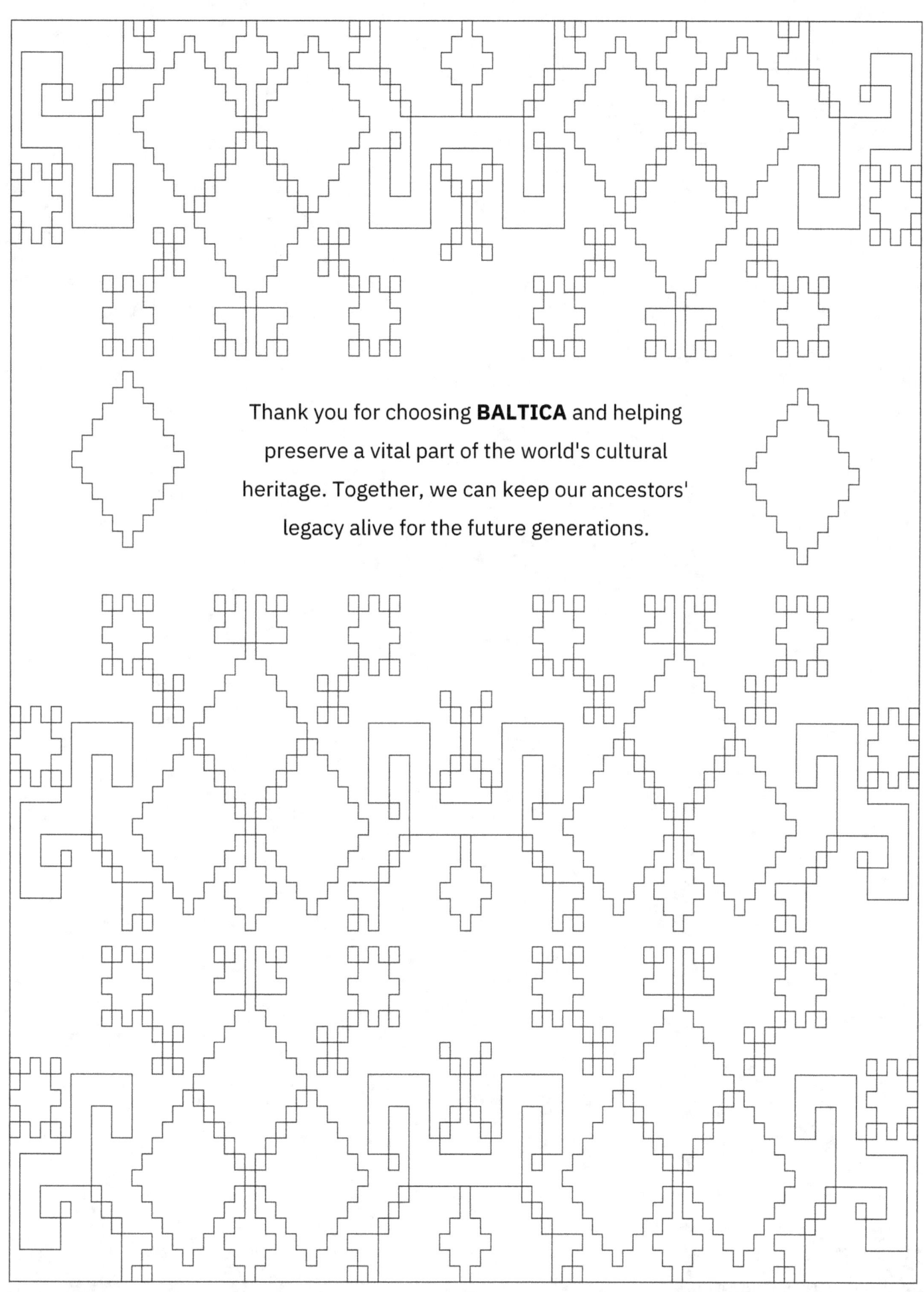

Thank you for choosing **BALTICA** and helping preserve a vital part of the world's cultural heritage. Together, we can keep our ancestors' legacy alive for the future generations.